Little Bighorn

WINNING THE BATTLE,
LOSING THE WAR

LANDMARK EVENTS IN
NATIVE AMERICAN HISTORY

THE APACHE WARS
The Final Resistance

BLACK HAWK AND THE WAR OF 1832
Removal in the North

CODE TALKERS AND WARRIORS
Native Americans and World War II

KING PHILIP'S WAR
The Conflict Over New England

LITTLE BIGHORN
Winning the Battle, Losing the War

THE LONG WALK
The Forced Navajo Exile

RED POWER
The Native American Civil Rights Movement

THE TRAIL OF TEARS
Removal in the South

Little Bighorn
WINNING THE BATTLE, LOSING THE WAR

MICHAEL L. LAWSON

SERIES EDITOR: PAUL C. ROSIER
Assistant Professor of History
Villanova University

CHELSEA HOUSE
PUBLISHERS
An imprint of Infobase Publishing

Cover: The Battle of the Little Bighorn is depicted in this 1889 lithograph by the Chicago firm Kurz and Allison.

LITTLE BIGHORN: Winning the Battle, Losing the War

Chelsea House
An imprint of Infobase Publishing
132 West 31st Street
New York NY 10001

Library of Congress Cataloging-in-Publication Data
Lawson, Michael L.
Little Bighorn : winning the battle, losing the war / Michael L. Lawson.
    p. cm. — (Landmark events in Native American history)
Includes bibliographical references and index.
ISBN-13: 978-0-7910-9347-4 (hardcover)
ISBN-10: 0-7910-9347-6 (hardcover)
1. Little Bighorn, Battle of the, Mont., 1876. I. Title. II. Series.
E83.876.L343 2007
973.8'2—dc22   2007000991

Chelsea House books are available at special discounts when purchased in bulk quantities for businesses, associations, institutions, or sales promotions. Please call our Special Sales Department in New York at (212) 967-8800 or (800) 322-8755.

You can find Chelsea House on the World Wide Web at
http://www.chelseahouse.com

Series design by Erika K. Arroyo
Cover design by Ben Peterson
Illustrations by Sholto Ainslie

Printed in the United States of America

Bang NMSG 10 9 8 7 6 5 4 3 2 1

This book is printed on acid-free paper.

All links and Web addresses were checked and verified to be correct at the time of publication. Because of the dynamic nature of the Web, some addresses and links may have changed since publication and may no longer be valid.

Contents

1 Warrior Nations 7

2 Differing Concepts of War 17

3 The Warpath to the Little Bighorn 28

4 Problems in the Unceded Territory 39

5 Custer's Offensive 51

6 Success of the Counterattack 62

7 Custer Rides the Ridges 74

8 The Battalion Disintegrates 85

9 The Road to Wounded Knee, 1876–1890 103

10 The Legacy of Little Bighorn 129

Chronology and Timeline 144

Notes 149

Bibliography 151

Further Reading 155

Index 159

Warrior Nations

ON THE HOT SUNDAY AFTERNOON OF JUNE 25, 1876, THE U.S. Army suffered the worst defeat of all of its battles with Native Americans. A great concentration of allied Sioux (pronounced like the name Sue) and Northern Cheyenne (pronounced like Shy Ann) warriors successfully turned back a surprise attack on their village near the Little Bighorn River in southeastern Montana. Women and children filled the native encampment, composed mostly of Sioux tribal members. Mounted on horseback, the troops of the U.S. Army's 7th Cavalry regiment launched the assault, which soon turned into a complete disaster for the soldiers.

Killed in the intense but relatively short battle was Lieutenant Colonel George Armstrong Custer, the colorful and controversial commanding officer of the regiment. Also killed in the conflict were 267 of the men under his command. The responding force of Native American warriors pinned down the remaining soldiers of the regiment on a nearby hilltop until the next day. By the time additional cavalry troops arrived on June 27 to rescue their comrades,

The Battle of the Little Bighorn, or *Peji Sluta* (Greasy Grass), as it is known in the Lakota dialect of the Sioux language, was the worst defeat suffered by the U.S. Army at the hands of a Native American opponent. The battle, which was fought on June 25, 1876, is depicted here by artist Feodor Fuchs in the inaccurately titled "Custer's Last Charge."

the Native Americans had gathered their families and rapidly departed.

This military disaster for the United States became known the world over as the Battle of the Little Bighorn. But the victorious Native American tribes that participated in the conflict remember it as the Battle of the *Peji Sluta*. Translated into English as "Greasy Grass," this is the name of the Little Bighorn River in the Lakota dialect of the Sioux language.

The fight at Greasy Grass was a great tactical victory for the warriors and the families they fought to protect. It represented the symbolic peak of their military power and their freedom to continue to use their hunting grounds. Yet, at the same time, the battle set in motion a series of negative events for the Sioux and their allies. Within a few years, these developments resulted in the ultimate strategic defeat of these Native American warrior nations and the loss of much of their traditional culture.

The citizens of the United States, who in 1876 counted only a few Native Americans among their number, were shocked and outraged when news of the Little Bighorn battle reached them. How, they wondered, could a commander and a military unit thought to be among America's best have suffered such a spectacular loss? The federal government also demanded to know why and how the disaster took place and who was to blame.

The search for answers to these questions has led to more than 130 years of controversy, speculation, and debate. The result is that Little Bighorn has become the most studied battle in American history, with the possible exception of the Civil War conflict at Gettysburg, Pennsylvania, in 1863. The unsolved mysteries and conflicting evidence and explanations regarding the Montana battle continue to fascinate and challenge all who study it closely.

The battalion that Custer personally led into the attack, a smaller unit of the overall cavalry regiment, became isolated in a separate section of the battleground. This area included a knoll, now known as Last Stand Hill, where the commander and 210 of his men were encircled and killed.

Reconstructing the precise events surrounding the defeat of Custer's battalion has been complicated by the fact that no soldiers survived that part of the battle. Native American participants were the only eyewitnesses. Many tribal members shared their memories of the Custer battle in later years. Yet, people who did not understand or appreciate the native cultural perspective generally dismissed these accounts as unbelievable or contradictory.

At the time, reporters chose to focus on the Little Bighorn battle as a national military defeat for the United States rather than as a Native American victory. In addition, historians would continue to focus on the defeat for several decades after the battle. In the absence of solid evidence, the need to bring closure to the event led to the gradual development of a heroic myth about the battle. In the version of the story that became popular in legend, the commander of the

LIEUTENANT COLONEL GEORGE ARMSTRONG CUSTER: U.S. ARMY COMMANDER AT LITTLE BIGHORN

George Armstrong Custer (1838–1876), the 7th Cavalry's flamboyant commander, was a national hero and the most popular soldier in the United States on the eve of the Little Bighorn battle. Born in New Rumley, Ohio, a distant relative of George Washington, he graduated at the bottom of the U.S. Military Academy's class of 1861 and was nearly expelled. However, he proved himself a gallant cavalry officer during the Civil War, capturing the first Confederate battle flag, leading electrifying charges at Gettysburg and elsewhere, and becoming the U.S. Army's youngest temporary general at age 23. Following the war, Custer participated in several conflicts with Native American tribes and sought to become America's premier "Indian fighter." The most controversial of these battles was the dawn attack he led in 1868 against Black Kettle's Cheyenne village near Oklahoma's Washita River, in which perhaps 100 villagers, mostly old men, women, and children, and 900 of their horses were massacred.

cavalry was cast as a heroic but doomed figure who bravely stood his ground until the end. This alleged defensive battle became famously known as "Custer's Last Stand." Likewise, Sioux war leaders, such as Crazy Horse and Gall, were heralded as military geniuses for leading warriors in decisive "charges" against U.S. Army positions.

In recent years, however, new evidence and interpretations have challenged many of the popularly held historical assumptions about the Little Bighorn battle. Archeological field studies have uncovered extensive new physical evidence from the battlefield. This evidence has helped pinpoint the location and size of the opposing forces at various stages of the battle. It has also provided a detailed inventory of the kinds and amounts of weapons and ammunition that were used. Among other findings, the patterns revealed by the artifacts suggest that the battle position of Custer's battalion collapsed much too quickly to be characterized as a "last stand."

Historians have also conducted more careful evaluations of the testimonies and perspectives of the Native American participants of the battle. This research has likewise led to new conclusions. The freshly interpreted evidence reveals, for example, that there were many Native American heroes and heroines in the battle. It also shows that some of the legendary heroic roles of Crazy Horse and Gall, assigned to them largely on the basis of their own self-promotion, are not supported by the eyewitness accounts of their fellow tribal members.

This short history of the Battle of the Little Bighorn places it in the context of the overall confrontation between two strong military forces during the latter half of the nineteenth century. On one side were the warrior nations of the Sioux and their allies, the conquerors of the northern plains. Pitted against these Native Americans was the professional army of a rising world power, the United States. Where possible, this book reflects Native American perspectives on the events that took place during the Sioux war years from 1851 to 1891. It also tries to project a more accurate history of the Little Bighorn battle itself. This approach is attempted by weaving together the most reliable sources from the past with evidence and interpretations produced by more recent historical and archeological research.

THE WARRIOR CULTURES OF THE SIOUX NATION AND ITS ALLIES

Before Europeans and Africans arrived in America, a large group of people identified collectively as the Sioux resided primarily in the lakes region around the headwaters of the Mississippi River in Minnesota. These people comprised a Native American nation because they shared a similar religion, culture, and language. They were not a nation in the sense of having an overall political or military structure or national leadership.

Each tribe within the nation operated independently, yet they shared a unity of spirit based on intermarriage, similar customs, and common historical experiences, including warfare. The Sioux Nation had no coordinated policy of conquest; neither did all of the Sioux tribes ever unite in battle against any enemy. It was not uncommon, however, for the tribes to form temporary alliances to face a common foe.

The warrior values and skills developed by the Sioux made the nation a major Native American military power on the Great Plains by the nineteenth century. During the nearly 200 years between 1685 and 1876, the westernmost Sioux tribe (the Lakota, described in more detail in the next chapter) conquered and controlled a vast area. The Sioux pushed many tribes out of their homelands and made others subject to their control. The Sioux territory of conquest expanded from the Minnesota River in modern-day Minnesota west to the headwaters of the Yellowstone River in

As the Sioux moved out on to the Great Plains in the eighteenth century, they drove many plains tribes farther west, including the Blackfeet. In this painting by American artist Charles M. Russell, Sioux warriors attack a Blackfeet warrior.

northwestern Wyoming. From there it stretched as far south as the upper Republican River in southwestern Nebraska.

The Sioux fought other Native American tribes for the social and economic advantages to be gained from obtaining resources such as horses, furs, slaves, and bigger and better hunting grounds. Increasingly after the middle of the nineteenth century, the Sioux also fought U.S. settlers and soldiers in order to protect their families, territory, resources, and freedom.

The Sioux and their allies were successful as warrior nations because they continually adapted to technological and economic changes. After acquiring guns from French traders in the late seventeenth century, the more western Sioux tribes pushed other Native Americans out of the prairie region east of the Missouri River. These Sioux then dominated the beaver trapping and fur trading industry in that area. By at least 1707, the Sioux also traded for horses. The Spanish had introduced these previously unknown animals to tribes in the American Southwest in the sixteenth century.

The Sioux and their allies successfully adapted the use of guns and special breeds of strong ponies to the pursuits of both hunting and combat. Mounted mobility gave them the advantage of quick attacks and getaways. Obtaining horses also made it easier and more profitable for them to pursue the roaming buffalo herds.

These innovations profoundly changed the lives of the Sioux people. The changes eventually shaped for them a no-madic way of life centered on the buffalo, their economic equivalent of a supermarket. These remarkable animals provided for most of the basic material needs of the tribes, including food, clothing, and shelter. The surplus hides, meat, and other buffalo byproducts were traded for guns and a wide variety of other Euro-American manufactured goods. The Sioux, Cheyennes, and Arapahos became com-paratively prosperous on the abundance made possible by the buffalo.

The pressure of constantly being hunted drove the buffalo to regions west and north of the Missouri River. The western, or Teton Sioux followed the herds across the Dakotas and into Montana and Wyoming. They raided and dominated the tribes native to these areas, and they did so because their successful buffalo economy depended on warfare to obtain additional horses for the hunt.

Like the Teton Sioux, the Cheyennes were also a people who gradually migrated westward from Minnesota to pursue the buffalo herds. They moved to the Black Hills of western South Dakota in the late eighteenth century, in part to avoid the aggressive Sioux tribes. From their base in the Black Hills, the Cheyennes fought tribes to the west for the control of hunting grounds in Montana, Wyoming, and Colorado.

By 1806, the Cheyennes had formed an alliance with the Arapahos in an attempt to counter the westward expansion of the Sioux. The Arapahos at that time ranged primarily between the North Platte River (in western Nebraska and eastern Wyoming) and the Arkansas River (in western Kansas and eastern Colorado). By 1826, the Cheyennes and Arapahos had entered into an uneasy alliance with the Sioux. The three nations fought against common enemies, but continued to compete against each other for the same buffalo hunting groups.

By the mid-nineteenth century, both the Cheyennes and the Arapahos separated into northern and southern divisions. The Southern Cheyennes and Southern Arapahos moved farther down the Arkansas River to Kansas and Oklahoma and became linked politically. The Northern Arapahos, then based primarily in Wyoming, tried to remain independent of the Northern Cheyennes and Sioux. In 1868, however, the U.S. government created a Great Sioux Reservation in western South Dakota. All of the Teton Sioux, Northern Cheyennes, and Northern Arapahos were eventually assigned to this reservation. Up until 1876, these tribes continued to hold the right to hunt buffalo on their traditional lands in Wyoming and Montana.

Warfare was a constant way of life for the Teton Sioux and their tribal allies. Success in personal combat provided the key path for a man to gain social status. The most honorable duty a man could perform was to fight an enemy. Female family members shared and enjoyed the status earned by successful warriors. Village communities fully participated in the preparations for combat. They celebrated the return of successful war parties and helped families mourn the loss of loved ones killed in battle.

Warfare was also morally justified by Sioux religious beliefs. The most sacred story of the origin of the Lakota, the westernmost Sioux tribe, is that of White Buffalo Calf

Woman giving the Sioux the gift of the Buffalo Calf Pipe. Smoking the pipe was an act of prayer in response to which the spirits would provide sufficient buffalo. White Buffalo Calf Woman taught the people the fundamentals and sacred rituals of their way of life. In doing so, she instructed them to fight their enemies and to consider any act in war to be a positive deed.

The Sioux concept of war emphasized individual acts of bravery. Such acts were encouraged and reinforced through a system of war honors, called *coups* in English. Counting coup on an enemy was based generally on the idea of touching the body of a fallen foe. The first four warriors to do so gained the honors of counting first, second, third, and fourth coup. Scalping the enemy (removing the scalp and hair with a knife or other sharp blade) also brought significant war honors. The highest ranking of honors involved killing a foe in hand-to-hand combat. Lesser honors could be earned by other acts, including stealing horses and kidnapping children.

Every aspect of Sioux warfare was surrounded in spiritual rituals. The emphasis on individual conduct and the spiritual nature of warfare made the methods of Sioux war parties very different than those used by Euro-American fighting forces. The methods of the U.S. Army emphasized the fighting group rather than the individual fighter. Military training focused on standardization, established tactics, and rules of battle, including following orders.

Differing Concepts of War

In comparison to U.S. Army soldiers, Sioux warriors did not have to follow any other tribesman, either on or off the field of battle. If enough warriors assembled around a recognized war leader, he might launch a tactical move. But when they had an opportunity to gain war honors, Sioux warriors could engage an enemy based on their own judgment. Recognized leaders could influence combat behavior, but warriors were not compelled to follow or even acknowledge their command.

There were no complex designs or war plans. The general pattern of engagement involved encircling the enemy, sneaking through enemy lines, sniping from behind natural barriers, and chasing those attempting to escape. Warriors tried to avoid being drawn into open combat. They commonly retreated in the face of unfavorable odds. They also withdrew from battle plans if they perceived any spiritual signs or omens of death or other negative events.

Sioux boys were trained at an early age in horsemanship and combat weaponry. Once they gained experience,

Like the Sioux, Cheyenne culture revolved around warfare and the need to protect their vast hunting grounds on the Great Plains. To that end, the horse became an integral part of Cheyenne and Sioux society. Three Cheyenne warriors on horseback are captured here by renowned frontier photographer Edward S. Curtis.

young men could join tribal warrior societies. Such organizations were not fighting units, but served rather to idealize and honor warfare. In this regard, they were similar to the Euro-American veterans' organizations. Their members had distinctive insignias, costumes, dances, and chants. They gathered at tribal events to boast of their combat achievements and war honors.

The war party was the basic fighting unit of Sioux warfare. Any warrior could propose the formation of a war party by declaring his cause or mission and inviting friends and family members to join him. Such proposals were subject to the approval of the local council of leaders. If the council endorsed a war expedition, other warriors could join the party.

The overall leader of a war party appointed veteran warriors to serve as his war leaders. They in turn appointed soldier leaders to keep the party organized and serve as scouts. Boys or young men on their first expedition served as water carriers. Their task was to perform the sometimes dangerous duty of obtaining water from sources near to where the party encamped.

The warrior cultures of the Sioux, Cheyenne, and Arapaho were similar in many respects. Each developed from the necessity of acquiring more horses, guns, and territory in order to exploit the abundant resources of the wandering buffalo. Each also had a similar system of war honors, men's organizations, religious ceremonies, and community activities that prepared tribal members mentally, spiritually, and physically for the challenges of the violent world of warfare.

THE WARRIOR CULTURE OF THE UNITED STATES

The United States was also a warrior nation. A little more than a decade before the Battle of the Little Bighorn, it had been fully engaged in the bloodiest and most destructive war known to the nation at that time. The Civil War that ended in 1865 took a mighty toll on the nation, in lives and resources, but also emotionally. Americans were weary of war, and the federal government was no longer willing to support a large military establishment. The size of the U.S. Army was cut in half between 1869 and 1874. Severe reductions in military budgets made a soldier's life difficult. Equipment of any kind was always in short supply. Army-issued food rations lacked both nutrition and taste. Uniforms were uncomfortable in most kinds of weather and completely inadequate for extreme conditions. Medical services were primitive at best.

Most young men had lost the sense of mission that had motivated them to volunteer in the fight to save the Union. Those who joined the U.S. Army in the post–Civil War era were driven more by lack of opportunities in civilian life than by patriotism or a sense of duty. While Sioux warriors held the highest prestige within their communities, most U.S. civilians looked down upon regular army soldiers as being inferior. All of the men in the U.S. Army were professional soldiers. (There were no women.) Soldiers either gained commissions as officers or enlisted to serve a set number of years. Cavalry recruits enlisted for five years with pay starting at $13 per month. The U.S. forces were drawn from various social and economic backgrounds, but did not generally represent the best and brightest of the population of young adult males. The U.S. Army's ranks tended to be overrepresented by unskilled workers and the urban poor. They also contained a significant number of foreign-born immigrants, especially from Ireland and Germany.

Although many African-American men served in the U.S. Army, they did so in segregated units under the command of white officers. The black regiments, the members of which named themselves "buffalo soldiers," served with distinction on the American frontier. Yet they were still the constant target of racial prejudice and discrimination. None of these units were present at the Little Bighorn.

Native Americans were employed by the U.S. Army to serve as scouts. These mercenaries worked as guides, trackers, and spies against other Native Americans. They sometimes also functioned as supplemental combat units. The so-called "Indian scouts" usually worked against the interests of tribes that were enemies of their own tribal groups. A few even worked in opposition to their own tribal people.

The 7th Cavalry was guided to the Little Bighorn village by a group of 35 scouts. Included in this group were 25 members of the Arikara tribe and 6 members of the Crow tribe.

Both of these tribes were longtime enemies of the Sioux. Five men of Sioux origin were also numbered among the regiment's scouts. Most of the 7th Cavalry's scouts did not take part in the combat at Little Bighorn. Minton "Mitch" Bouyer was the only scout who died with Custer's battalion. Bouyer was the son of a Sioux woman and a French trader and had been adopted into the Crow tribe.

U.S. Army officers consisted mostly of a mixture of graduates of the U.S. Military Academy at West Point, New York, and veterans who had volunteered to serve during the Civil War. They were paid much less than they could have earned in civilian jobs. Promotions were slow in coming and most officers held the same rank for many years. Competition for the limited opportunities for advancement generated a good deal of petty bickering among officers.

The U.S. Army's battle tactics were dictated in standard textbooks. For example, the cavalry operated under a tactical manual written by Emory Upton in 1874. The basic tactic was the use of a skirmish line of mounted troops or foot soldiers spread five yards apart. These skirmishers engaged the enemy with firepower while other line and column formations were deployed. To "deploy a unit" was to establish a battle formation or position. Upton's manual also included instructions for launching a mounted charge in a surprise attack. The cavalry at Little Bighorn used both of these tactics.

The company was the basic tactical fighting unit of the cavalry at the battle. There were 12 companies in the 7th Cavalry. Each company contained 40 to 59 men under the command of a captain or first lieutenant. Companies were organized into battalions of various sizes. Custer was the overall commander of the regiment, but the unit that he personally led into battle was a battalion consisting of 5 companies. It was this unit that was completely wiped out on Last Stand Hill. A platoon was a smaller unit of a company, usually consisting of 8 to 10 soldiers. A platoon might be organized for special tasks, such as scouting or escorting, or to deploy where a full company's strength was not needed.

Despite the poor conditions in the U.S. Army, military units maintained a sense of pride and spirit. The 7th Cavalry was an especially prideful group that considered itself an elite unit. This reflected in part the attitude and showiness of its commander. Army men bonded together through common experiences and familiarity. The distinctive characteristics and traditions of their units helped to mold loyalty and solidarity. They had, for example, a distinctive regimental swallow-tailed flag, called a guidon, which they carried on a staff whenever the troops rode together. The 7th Cavalry also adopted as its regimental battle song an old Irish quickstep tune called "Garry Owen."

Unlike young Native American warriors, U.S. Army recruits did not receive extensive training in either horsemanship or marksmanship. The daily routine for meals, supplies, maintenance, and guard duty did not allow adequate time for such training. Neither did the U.S. Army supply its men with the best weapons and horses available. Budget cuts severely limited even the amount of ammunition that could be used for target practice. The U.S. Army had a high turnover rate because the conditions of service were so unappealing. The loss of soldiers whose terms had expired, combined with the lack of training, meant that there was always a high proportion of inexperienced men in the ranks. All of these factors proved to be disadvantages for the U.S. Army at the Battle of the Little Bighorn.

THE PEOPLE OF THE LITTLE BIGHORN VILLAGE

The name *Sioux* was derived from a French garbling of an Ojibwa word used in a negative sense to convey the meaning "little snakes." The Ojibwa, or Chippewa, lived to the east of the Sioux in the Minnesota area and were one of their traditional tribal enemies. The people commonly called Sioux prefer to be known by a name that means "allies" in one of the three dialects of the Siouan language. These are the names *Dakota*, *Nakota*, and *Lakota*. In addition to reflecting different dialects, these names are also used to describe the distinct divisions, regions, and economies of the traditional Sioux Nation of the nineteenth century.

Prior to contact with Euro-Americans, the Sioux Nation was made up of seven divisions known as the Seven Council Fires. The Dakota consisted of four divisions: the Mdewakanton, Wahpeton, Wahpekute, and Sisseton. The members of these four divisions became better known as the Santee. They resided in the eastern and northeastern portion of the traditional territory used and occupied by the Sioux, primarily in the lakes region of Minnesota. Most of their economy was based on fishing, harvesting wild rice, and gathering herbs.

The Nakota consisted of two divisions: the Yankton and the Yanktonai. They used and occupied an area to the southwest of the Dakotas, primarily in southern Minnesota. Their economy was distinct from the other Sioux in that it was centered on the quarrying of pipestone, a unique rock used to make ceremonial smoking pipes.

The Lakota comprised only one division of the nation, but themselves consisted of seven subdivisions, or bands. The Lakota economy, and indeed much of its culture, centered on the hunting and harvesting of buffalo. By the nineteenth century, they came to reside to the northwest, west, and southwest of the Dakotas on the plains of present-day western North and South Dakota and eastern Montana and Wyoming. The seven bands are identified here by the Lakota, French, or English names by which they are most commonly known. The Oglala, the largest band, lived in the southwest portion of this region. The next most populous band, the Brulé, lived to the southeast of the Oglalas. The Minneconjou and Two Kettle bands lived north of the Brulés. The Hunkpapa,

Sans Arc, and Black Foot (not to be confused with the Black-feet confederacy of northwestern Montana) were smaller Lakota bands that occupied the northwestern region of the Sioux Nation's territory. The Lakotas were also identified historically by non-Indians as the Teton, or western Sioux. During the last generation, these terms have fallen out of use in favor of *Lakota,* the name by which the people prefer to be known.

Lakotas comprised the vast majority of tribal members attacked at Little Bighorn. Each tribal group encamped in the village in their own cluster of lodges or tepees. A tepee is a cone-shaped tent made by wrapping animal hides (now canvas) around long, wooden support poles. The word

CHIEF SITTING BULL (TATANKA IYOTANKA): LEADER OF THE LAKOTA

Sitting Bull (c. 1831–1890) was the charismatic Lakota spiritual and military leader who drew together at the Little Bighorn the Sioux, Northern Cheyenne, and Arapaho families that refused to stay on the Great Sioux Reservation. Born near the Grand River in South Dakota into a prominent Hunkpapa family, his father and two uncles were tribal chiefs and he and his two younger brothers also became chiefs. He killed a buffalo at age 10 and first counted coup (touching an enemy warrior in battle) on a Crow warrior at age 14. He battled U.S. troops for the first time in 1863 and fought them again in numerous other encounters between 1864 and 1872. In addition to gaining respect as a fierce warrior, he also became widely known for his spiritual powers. In 1869, a council of chiefs elected him to the unprecedented position of "supreme chief" of the Sioux Nation.

Brulé warrior Crow Dog, who is pictured here in 1900 at the age of 65, was one of the participants in the Battle of the Little Bighorn. Although Crow Dog did not kill anyone during the battle, his wife, One-Who-Walks-with-the-Stars, killed two soldiers who were attempting to swim across the river.

tepee is derived from the Lakota term *thipi*, meaning "house," or "dwelling."

When the tribes gathered on the open prairie for events such as the 1876 Sun Dance, each tribe clustered in its own distinct circle. At Little Bighorn, however, there was no need to form tribal circles. The organization of the tribal clusters was based on the travel order maintained along the trail, on family relationships, and on the geography of the site.

Oglala families occupied the greatest number of tepees in the Little Bighorn village. Their war chiefs in the camp included Crazy Horse, Big Road, Low Dog, American Horse, and He Dog. Next in number were the lodges in the Hunkpapa formation, including that of Sitting Bull, the spiritual leader who was the inspiration for so many people to lodge together at the Greasy Grass. The war chiefs of the Hunkpapa group included Gall, Black Moon, Crow King, and Rain in the Face. The Hunkpapa cluster also included a small number of Santees and Yanktonais (perhaps 25 tepees) led by Red on Top and Inkpaduta.

The Minneconjous, led by Red Horse, Lame Deer, Fast Bull, and Hump, occupied the third-largest Lakota cluster. A smaller number of Black Foot under Jumping Bear and Kill Eagle, and Brulés under Crow Dog, were encamped together with some Two Kettle families. Somewhat smaller still was the representation of the Sans Arcs under Spotted Eagle.

The Northern Cheyenne cluster completed the makeup of the village. This grouping also included a few Southern Cheyenne and Northern Arapaho tribal members. The Northern Cheyenne families at the Little Bighorn village were drawn there by the spiritual charisma of the Sioux religious leader Sitting Bull. They comprised about 14 percent of the total village population. Their leaders in camp included Lame White Man, Two Moon, and Old Bear. The individual tribes encamped in separate formations in the village.

Five Northern Arapaho hunters had wandered into the Little Bighorn village out of curiosity. The Lakotas treated them as prisoners, because most of the Northern Arapaho men had volunteered to serve in the U.S. Army as scouts against the Sioux and Northern Cheyennes. These Arapahos joined the battle to defend the village after it was attacked, but quickly slipped away once it was over.

The Warpath to the Little Bighorn

THE HISTORICAL WARPATH THAT LED THESE NATIVE Americans to their destiny at Little Bighorn was staked out 25 years earlier. By 1851, the alliance of the Sioux, Cheyenne, and Arapaho warrior nations dominated the northern and central plains. In that year, U.S. government commissioners held a conference near Fort Laramie (present-day Wyoming) with representatives of the Sioux, Cheyenne, Arapaho, and other Native American nations. This conference produced a treaty of peace with the United States that became known as the Fort Laramie Treaty of 1851. It established the boundaries of each tribe's territory and pledged that none of the parties would engage in war. In exchange for $50,000 in annuities (an annual payment of certain goods) during a period of 50 years, the Sioux agreed to allow the United States to establish roads and military posts within their territory. This agreement established the legal basis for the Oregon Trail that followed the Platte River through Sioux territory in Nebraska and Wyoming.

The treaty turned out to be irrelevant. Both Native Americans and the United States soon ignored the boundaries it created. The prohibition against intertribal warfare was disregarded by the warrior nation to which it was primarily meant to apply—the Sioux. The United States considered the treaty to apply to the entire Sioux Nation. Yet those Sioux tribes not represented in the negotiations, including the Hunkpapa and Black Foot, did not view the treaty as binding on them. The other tribes found it difficult to take the treaty seriously when, soon after it was put in place, the United States engaged in war against other tribes. The government also hedged on its obligations under the treaty when the U.S. Senate reduced the term of annuity payments from 50 to 15 years.

The real and lasting effect of the treaty was its establishment of a clear line of conflict between the Sioux and the United States. Prior to the Fort Laramie conference, these two warrior nations had advanced steadily on the frontier with little direct confrontation. After the treaty was in place, the nations became sworn enemies and very clearly recognized rivals for power. The first battle between the two expanding powers broke out within four years of the treaty. Armed conflict then continued periodically for more than three decades.

The Oregon Trail also created hostilities. Euro-Americans passing along the trail to the West spread disease to Native Americans and drove away the buffalo herds. Frequent negative contacts between Sioux tribal members and the wagon trains came to a crisis point in 1854. In August of that year, a Mormon emigrant on the trail complained to the U.S. Army at Fort Laramie that a tribal member of Chief Conquering Bear's nearby camp had killed his cow. The camp consisted of about 4,000 Brulés and Oglalas who had traveled to the area near the fort to receive their annuities.

The commanding officer at Fort Laramie decided to test the authority of Conquering Bear, whom the 1851 treaty commissioners had established as head chief of the entire Sioux Nation. He ordered Lieutenant John L. Grattan, a recent graduate of West Point, and a detachment of 29 soldiers of the 6th Infantry regiment to go to the Sioux camp and demand the surrender of the suspect.

High Forehead, a Minneconjou visitor to the Sioux camp, was the man thought to be guilty. Since Conquering Bear was in reality only a leader of the Brulés, he could not compel this member of another Sioux tribe to give himself up. The precise details of the events that followed are not known for sure, but growing tensions led to gunfire. The soldiers, whose firepower included two howitzer cannons, assassinated Conquering Bear. In response, the warriors in camp killed Grattan and all of his men. This event, which sparked years of conflict between the Sioux and the United States, became known to

GENERAL WILLIAM SELBY HARNEY: PEACE NEGOTIATOR

William Selby Harney (1800–1898) was one of the best-known military figures in the United States during the era before the Civil War. Born in Haysborough, Tennessee, he was commissioned at age 17 as a non-West Point second lieutenant in the U.S. 1st Infantry. In his 45 years of active duty, during which he rose to the rank of major general, he participated in many conflicts against Native Americans. These included the Creek wars, the Black Hawk War, the Second Seminole War, and the largest and most successful pre-Civil War campaign against the Sioux. He was acclaimed for his humane ideas about how to treat Native Americans and was respected by many native leaders. Yet he also had a reputation for brutality and violations of the articles of war, including accusations of raping and murdering Native American women. He was a leading member of the peace commission that negotiated the Fort Laramie Treaty of 1868.

Euro-Americans as the Grattan Massacre. Native Americans, however, remember it as the "War of the Mormon Cow."

The Sioux learned the lesson that day that the U.S. Army was capable of unprovoked attacks on Native American people. One young man, an Oglala named Crazy Horse, was especially influenced by the incident. Soon after the battle, he had a vision that revealed his destiny to serve as a war chief. From then on he played a significant role in many battles, including the defense of the Little Bighorn village.

To avenge the murder of Conquering Bear, Brulé warriors began attacking wagon trains on the Oregon Trail. In November 1854, a war party killed three people on a mail wagon. In response to these hostilities, the U.S. Army sent Brigadier General William S. Harney to lead a military campaign against the Sioux. Harney commanded the 2nd Mounted Dragoons, a unit that was renamed the 2nd Cavalry regiment at the beginning of the Civil War. In September 1855, Harney and his 600 troops rode along the Oregon Trail in search of the Sioux. They discovered and attacked the Brulé village headed by Little Thunder, the leader who had succeeded Conquering Bear. This encampment was located on Blue Water Creek near Ash Hollow in southwestern Nebraska.

Although Little Thunder's village had not been involved in the Grattan affair, the U.S. Army killed 86 of its tribal members. The Sioux witnessed for the first time the slaughter of their women and children by soldiers of the United States. In addition, Harney ordered the capture of 70 Brulé women and children, who were then marched to a military post in present-day South Dakota. This military strike became popularly known as the Battle of Ash Hollow, or the Battle of Blue Water Creek. Historically, Euro-Americans only described such acts of violence as "massacres" when they were the victims.

Following the attack, Harney and his mounted troops made a wide sweep through the surrounding Sioux territory.

They made no further attacks, however, and were not challenged by the Sioux. Perhaps as a result of Harney's actions, the Oregon Trail remained relatively free from Sioux attacks for another decade.

In April 1856, Harney brought representatives of the various Sioux tribes together at Fort Pierre, South Dakota, to negotiate a treaty. As a goodwill gesture, a Minneconjou leader surrendered High Forehead, the killer of the Mormon cow. Harney secured an agreement from the Sioux that they would not attack other tribes or Euro-Americans crossing their territory.

The Sioux leaders were impressed with the conference, and the agreement it produced might have eventually had a positive impact. However, the Office of Indian Affairs (OIA) objected to the terms negotiated by Harney. The OIA, part of the U.S. Department of the Interior, had the primary responsibility for Native American matters, whereas General Harney represented the U.S. War Department. As a result, the U.S. Senate refused to ratify the treaty. As happened so often throughout the nineteenth century, the Sioux were caught between the conflicting policies of the civilian and military branches of the U.S. government.

At the Fort Pierre conference, General Harney again tried to name a head chief of the entire Sioux Nation. The government commonly tried to prop up a national leader to be a spokesperson for all of the tribes, but this concept and position was completely unfamiliar to the Sioux. Harney named the Hunkpapa leader Bear Ribs to replace the murdered Conquering Bear as head chief of the Sioux Nation.

The Sioux were divided over the issue of whether they should accept the annuity goods provided as payments by the Fort Laramie Treaty of 1851. For example, the young men of the Hunkpapa and Black Foot tribes were strongly opposed to accepting these goods because no representative of their tribes had agreed to the terms of the treaty. In 1862, when

In 1851, the Santee Sioux, who largely lived in present-day Minnesota, signed the Treaty of Traverse de Sioux with the U.S. government. Under the terms of the treaty, the Santees agreed to give up all their lands in southern and western Minnesota Territory, along with some lands in Iowa and Dakota territories in return for $1,665,000 in cash and annuities.

Bear Ribs defied these opponents and accepted the annuity goods, a Sans Arc tribal member assassinated him. After that incident, the United States never again tried to appoint a "head chief" of the Sioux Nation.

To the east, the Santee Sioux in Minnesota entered into separate treaties with the United States in 1851. By the terms of the treaties of Traverse de Sioux and Mendota, they gave up rights to all their lands in Minnesota and the Dakotas. In return, they were promised annuity payments and an area of reserved land. In 1858, the Santees were pressured into signing a treaty for the sale of even more lands.

THE SIOUX WARS OF THE 1850s AND 1860s

Euro-American settlers rapidly surrounded the Santee people and constantly tried to cheat them and obtain more of their lands. Factions within the tribes were divided over whether they should accept the situation or retaliate. In August 1862, four young warriors forced the issue by killing five Euro-American settlers following a minor incident. This confrontation quickly exploded into a widespread war that became known as the Minnesota Sioux Uprising. The Santee leader Little Crow, who previously had been an advocate of peace, organized parties totaling 700 warriors. The war parties raided trading posts and settlements, including the village of New Ulm. Their attacks resulted in the death of 1,000 Euro-Americans, including 23 infantrymen of the U.S. Army.

The Santee attack on the U.S. Army camp at Wood Lake on September 23, 1862, proved to be the turning point of the war. General Henry B. Sibley, later Minnesota's first governor, commanded the unit. The U.S. Army's superior artillery fire scattered the 700 warriors in defeat. Many of the surviving fighters fled to find refuge with other Sioux tribes in Dakota Territory. These included bands of Sissetons, Yanktonais, and Lakotas. Others followed Little Crow into Canada.

The 303 warriors who stayed in Minnesota surrendered peacefully and gave up their captives. Still, a U.S. military court sentenced them all to death by hanging. President Abraham Lincoln reduced the sentence for all but 38 of these Santee Sioux prisoners. On December 26, 1862, the unpardoned tribal members were simultaneously hanged at Mankato, Minnesota. This event was the largest mass execution ever carried out by the government of the United States.

Settlers then murdered Little Crow, the leader of the uprising, in July 1863. He was at the time leading a horse-stealing party from Canada back into Minnesota. By that time, local governments were paying bounties for Sioux scalps. In August 1863, the U.S. Army launched a punitive expedition against the Santees who fled into North Dakota. General Sibley led one column northeast out of Minnesota, while General Alfred Sully led another column up the Missouri River. This campaign marked the beginning of an almost continuous period of warfare between the United States and the Sioux tribes. The conflict would continue until the surrender of Sitting Bull and his warriors in 1881.

At the battles of Big Mound, Dead Buffalo Lake, and Stony Lake in south-central North Dakota, General Sibley's

RED CLOUD (MAKHPIYA-LUTA): OGLALA LEADER

Red Cloud (1822–1909) was the most successful Native American military leader in conflicts against the United States. Attacks he launched during Red Cloud's War (1866–68) compelled the U.S. government to abandon its Bozeman Trail forts and guaranteed the Sioux possession of their own territory. Born near the forks of the North Platte River in Nebraska, Red Cloud was the son of an Oglala mother and a Brulé father. After Red Cloud's father died, he was raised in the household of Chief Smoke, his maternal uncle. At age 19, he killed one of his uncle's rivals, an event that divided the Oglalas for half a century. Red Cloud then gained prominence for his leadership in territorial conflicts with rival tribes. He remained an important Oglala leader following the Fort Laramie Treaty, but settled on the reservation and chose not to become associated with Sitting Bull in 1876 or with the Ghost Dance religion in 1890.

forces defeated Santee refugees and their Hunkpapa and Black Foot protectors. It is likely that Sitting Bull and other tribal members later present at Little Bighorn took part in these battles. In September 1863 and in July 1864, General Sully's command defeated similar coalitions of Nakota, Dakota, and Lakota Sioux warriors at Whitestone Hill in southeastern North Dakota and in the Killdeer Mountains in western North Dakota. The latter conflict marked the first battle for 14-year-old White Bull, a nephew of Sitting Bull, who was also a participant in this losing battle. White Bull would become one of the most distinguished war leaders at Little Bighorn. Both the Santees and their allied Sioux Nation defenders paid a dear price for the uprising in Minnesota.

By 1863, while the Civil War raged in the East, Euro-American emigrants again challenged the Sioux Nation. The discovery of gold in Montana led to the establishment of the Bozeman Trail. This new roadway provided a shortcut to the gold fields from the Oregon Trail in Wyoming. It passed through the Sioux tribes' prime buffalo hunting grounds on the Powder River. Within four years, the U.S. Army constructed four military posts to protect the trail: Fort Reno, Fort Phil Kearny, Fort C. F. Smith, and Fort Fetterman.

This expansion into Sioux territory touched off a series of conflicts that became known as Red Cloud's War. As a leader of the Oglala, Red Cloud united warriors of the Lakota and other tribes in an effort to shut down the Bozeman Trail. Many younger war leaders who would later take part in the Battle of the Little Bighorn supported him. These included the aspiring Oglala warrior Crazy Horse and the Hunkpapa fighter Rain in the Face. Between 1866 and 1868, Sioux war parties disrupted travelers along the trail and threatened the U.S. Army's four posts.

On December 21, 1866, Red Cloud and his warriors soundly defeated an army detachment near Fort Phil Kearny in north-central Wyoming. Commanded by Captain William

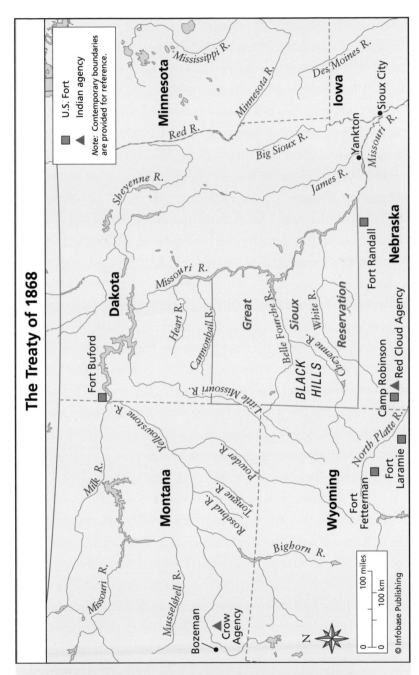

Under the terms of the Fort Laramie Treaty of 1868, the Sioux agreed to settle on the Great Sioux Reservation, a vast area of present-day South Dakota, west of the Missouri River. The reservation, along with the traditional Sioux territory, is depicted on this map.

J. Fetterman, the U.S. Army unit was lured into an ambush. Fetterman had once bragged that he and 80 good soldiers could defeat the entire Sioux Nation. As it turned out, the captain and exactly 80 of his men were killed in this fight.

In response, the U.S. Army launched another offensive campaign against the Sioux. By August 1867, U.S. troops managed to defeat warriors at the Wagon Box in north-central Wyoming and the Hayfield fight in south-central Montana. Despite these victories, the U.S. government began to realize that protecting the Bozeman Trail was a hopeless task. Besides, the construction of the Union Pacific railroad line through the area meant that the trail might no longer be necessary. As a result, the government decided to abandon its forts on the trail and negotiate a peace treaty.

In May 1868, Sioux representatives under the leadership of Red Cloud gathered at Fort Laramie, Wyoming, to discuss treaty terms with government agents. The shrewd Red Cloud refused to sign the treaty until after the Bozeman Trail forts were burned to the ground. He thus became the only Native American leader ever to wage war against the United States and succeed in winning concessions from the government.

The Fort Laramie Treaty of 1868 established a reserved area for the Teton Sioux called the Great Sioux Reservation. This area included all of present-day South Dakota west of the Missouri River. The treaty also recognized an area of "unceded Indian territory." This country was composed of land in Nebraska north of the Platte River and in eastern Wyoming and Montana from the western reservation boundary to the peaks of the Big Horn Mountains. The treaty recognized the right of the Sioux to continue to hunt buffalo on the North Platte and Republican rivers as long as the herds remained. It also required Euro-Americans to obtain tribal consent to enter the unceded territory. Their failure to do so would trigger a new round of conflicts.

Problems in the Unceded Territory

THE FORT LARAMIE TREATY OF 1868 INFLUENCED ALL future interactions between the Sioux and the United States, including the Battle of the Little Bighorn. The treaty provided for the payment of annuities for 30 years. These goods were to be distributed at agencies on the reservation, the first of which was established on the Missouri River. However, many if not most of the Teton Sioux chose to live in the unceded territory west of the reservation. In 1868, a large number of Lakotas occupied the Yellowstone River area. Along with many Yanktonais and Northern Cheyennes, the Lakotas were attracted to a hunting area that extended from the Yellowstone to the Missouri River and as far west as the Milk River in Montana. In this area, they pursued the last great buffalo herds. They also fought with all of the tribes native to the region for the right to do so. These included the Assiniboine, Blackfeet, Crow, Gros Ventre, and Shoshone.

The Sioux bands in the unceded territory intended to maintain their traditional nomadic culture. After Red Cloud and other leaders decided to resign themselves to life on the

By 1870, Sitting Bull, a Hunkpapa Sioux, had emerged as one of the prominent leaders of his people. An advocate of traditional culture and religion, Sitting Bull (pictured here in 1885) believed the Sioux should isolate themselves from the *wasichus,* or whites.

reservation, the wandering hunters sought new leadership. By 1870, a Hunkpapa named Sitting Bull emerged as their most inspirational and dominant leader. He had not been a particularly distinguished warrior or politician, but was instead a spiritual leader or "medicine man." He believed that the Lakota people and their allies should isolate themselves from the *wasichus* ("white eyes"), or Euro-Americans. He advised that they should strictly follow their traditional culture and religion.

A majority of tribal members responded to Sitting Bull's preaching and departed the reservation to continue their old ways in the unceded territory. Many of these people still went to the agencies in winter months to trade and receive annuity rations. Then they rejoined the hunting and raiding parties of the traditionalists.

It became increasingly difficult for Native Americans to maintain isolation and traditional ways in the unceded territory. Every year they saw fewer buffalo but more signs of Euro-American expansion. The 1868 treaty gave the United States the right to build a railroad line across present-day North Dakota and Montana. Sitting Bull and his followers opposed the construction of this Northern Pacific line and threatened to attack its surveying crews. The U.S. Army also increased its presence in the area. The Sioux responded by constantly attacking the military escorts assigned to protect railroad workers, but they were not able to halt construction of the line.

In the summer of 1874, the U.S. Army sent an expedition of 1,000 men under Lieutenant Colonel George Armstrong Custer to explore the Black Hills. This heavily forested region was on the western end of the Great Sioux Reservation, primarily within the border of modern-day South Dakota. The official mission of the expedition was to find a suitable location for a military post to monitor the Sioux. But the unofficial task of the party, which included mineral surveyors, was to investigate rumors of gold deposits in the area. Its confirmation of the presence of the mineral "in paying quantities" led to a rush of Euro-American gold seekers to the hills.

The U.S. government then attempted to purchase the Black Hills, but the Sioux and Northern Cheyenne considered the *Paha Sapa* (the hills that are black) to be a sacred area. The Lakotas believed it to be their place of creation. Sitting Bull and those he influenced spread the message that the Paha Sapa would not be sold or leased. The U.S. government was obliged to accept this position, but it did nothing to prevent more gold seekers from illegally entering the reservation.

It became clear to U.S. government officials that they urgently needed to address the problem of the Native American traditionalists in the unceded territory. The government also needed to stem the influence of Sitting Bull and his followers on the people of the reservation. The solution implemented by the Office of Indian Affairs on December 6, 1875, was to order all Sioux people to return to the reservation by January 31, 1876. If they did not, they would be considered "hostile." This meant that the U.S. Army would deal with them as an enemy force.

It was virtually impossible for the people to return to the reservation at that time of winter. Aside from that, they were not inclined to do so. The roamers were well supplied with buffalo meat, horses, and weapons and so they chose to ignore the government's order. A famine on the reservation at that same time convinced many other tribal members that they should join the roamers as soon as the weather improved.

After the deadline for return passed without a response, the government decided to let the U.S. Army get involved. The commander of the Division of the Missouri was General Phillip H. Sheridan, remembered for his racist remark that "the only good Indian is a dead Indian." Sheridan's immediate boss was William Tecumseh Sherman, the head general of the U.S. Army. Both men had been commanders under General Ulysses S. Grant during the Civil War. Now Grant was the president of the United States and the three men were in a position to dictate military solutions for problems involving Native Americans.

General Sheridan ordered his subordinate commanders, generals Alfred H. Terry and George Crook, to launch a campaign against the "hostiles." The mission was to converge on the encampments of the Sioux and Northern Cheyennes and force the Native Americans to return to the reservation. Their location was believed to be in the Big Horn Valley of Montana.

Hostile conflicts with the Sioux throughout the course of the previous decade had convinced the U.S. Army that winter campaigns were more likely to be successful. The tribes were

GENERAL GEORGE CROOK: NOTABLE INDIAN FIGHTER

George Crook (1828–1890) was considered to be the U.S. Army's greatest fighter of Native Americans. He earned a reputation for his respect of native people both on and off the battlefield. Born in Taylorsville, Ohio, to a farming family, Crook graduated near the bottom of the U.S. Military Academy's class of 1852. He saw extensive action during the Civil War, was promoted to the temporary rank of brigadier general, and was held as a Confederate prisoner of war for a month. After the war, he participated in campaigns against the Paiutes in the Pacific Northwest and the Apaches in Arizona. Facing the Sioux and Northern Cheyennes in 1876, his troops were forced to retreat from the Battle of the Rosebud. Following the war with the Sioux, he returned to Arizona to campaign against Geronimo, the Chiricahua Apache leader. According to Red Cloud, Crook "never lied to us. His words gave the people hope."

too elusive in other seasons. Sheridan's plan was to launch a winter campaign with three columns: Two columns were to be led by General Terry, commander of the Department of Dakota, and one by General Crook, commander of the Department of the Platte.

Only General Crook's troops managed to move toward the target area before the end of winter. General Terry's command was delayed by severe weather and supply problems. After 10 days on the move, General Crook sent six companies (300 men) to attack the village of the Northern Cheyenne leader Old Bear in the Powder River Valley of Montana. The Native American encampment contained 110 lodges and perhaps as many as 250 warriors. These included many who would later fight at Little Bighorn, including He Dog, Little Wolf, and Two Moon. The villagers managed to escape to nearby bluffs. The soldiers burned the village but did not accomplish their mission. The failure of this winter attack against a weaker force meant that a summer campaign would now be necessary.

The survivors of the Powder River battle later found refuge in the camp of the Oglala leader Crazy Horse. Their stories of the attack spread rapidly among the roamers. The news served as a clear warning that the U.S. Army was planning to wage total war against them. With the coming of spring, more of the scattered camps joined together for protection. Families that left the reservation in that season also swelled their numbers.

THE U.S. ARMY'S CENTENNIAL CAMPAIGN

By May 1876, the U.S. Army's three-column campaign was finally in the field. A column headed by Colonel John Gibbons headed east from Fort Shaw and Fort Ellis in Montana. This unit included 400 soldiers and 25 Crow scouts. General Terry's Dakota column headed west from Fort Abraham Lincoln near present-day Bismarck, North Dakota. His command consisted of 39 Arikara scouts and 900 soldiers, in addition to the 12 companies of the 7th Cavalry regiment under Custer. General Crook led the largest column, consisting of 1,000 soldiers, 80 armed civilians, and 260 Crow and Eastern Shoshone scouts. This unit moved northward from Fort Fetterman, Wyoming.

In early June 1876, a large group of Sioux and Northern Cheyennes gathered on the Rosebud Creek in Montana for their annual Sun Dance. This was their most important spiritual ritual. Sitting Bull was among the leaders at the gathering. After sacrificing 50 pieces of his flesh in the dance, he fell into a trance and experienced a graphic vision. After he regained consciousness, he told the people that he had seen many killed U.S. soldiers falling upside down into the Sioux village. This vision was taken as a prophecy of future success in battle against the soldiers they called the "Long Knives." They were given this name because of the long swords, or sabers, they carried with them. Following the Sun Dance, the camp moved southward and attracted more people as word spread of Sitting Bull's vision.

By June 11, 1876, General Crook's column had established a supply camp on Goose Creek, near present-day Sheridan, Wyoming. A group of Northern Cheyennes under Little Hawk monitored the column's movements. They reported the approach of the soldiers to the main encampment of Sioux and Northern Cheyennes at that time on Reno Creek.

Eager for action, the young war leaders at the main camp decided in an intertribal council meeting to launch a surprise attack on Crook's forces. On the morning of June 17, 1876, hundreds of warriors swarmed down on Crook's column as it approached a bend in Rosebud Creek. The Oglala fighter Crazy Horse led the attackers. The soldiers were surprised initially, but with the help of their Crow and Shoshone scouts, they were able to fight the warriors to a stalemate.

The Battle of the Rosebud ended when the warriors broke off fighting and returned to their camp. They had suffered fewer than 100 casualties. Among the U.S. soldiers, 10 had died and 21 were wounded. Alarmed by the aggressiveness and size of the war party, General Crook decided to return to the Goose Creek supply camp and wait for reinforcements. This decision sidelined his important force for more than seven weeks. Just before the most important battle of the war, which would take place about a week later at Little Bighorn, nearly half of General Sheridan's combat strength in the field was effectively taken out of the campaign.

Lieutenant Colonel Custer was supposed to command the Dakota column. This was the unit that was to move westward from Fort Abraham Lincoln in the spring of

CRAZY HORSE (TASUNKA WITKO): LAKOTA WARRIOR

Crazy Horse (c. 1842–1877) was the greatest of all Lakota warriors and one of the outstanding native leaders at the Battle of the Little Bighorn. He was born near Bear Butte on the eastern side of the Black Hills in South Dakota. His father was an Oglala war chief and his mother a Brulé. He rose rapidly in the warrior ranks of his tribe, gaining numerous honors in conflicts with enemy tribes. Beginning in 1864, he also played a key role in numerous conflicts with the frontier U.S. Army, including the 1866 Fetterman "Massacre," which resulted in the deaths of Captain William J. Fetterman and 80 U.S. soldiers. Although dazzling in battle, he was a quiet introvert and mystic prone to eccentric dress and unpredictable behavior. However, he lost his rank as a war chief in 1870 after being shot in the face while attempting to steal another warrior's wife. Determined to preserve the freedom of his people, he became one of Sitting Bull's staunchest allies.

In 1876, Lieutenant Colonel George Armstrong Custer was assigned the command of the 7th Cavalry unit within the Department of Dakota of the U.S. Army. On May 17 of that year, the Dakota column, including 12 companies of Custer's mounted regiment, left Fort Abraham Lincoln for the Powder River region of Montana to challenge the Sioux.

1876 to connect with Colonel Gibbons's Montana column and General Crook's Platte column. President Grant, however, suspended Custer from command on the eve of the campaign. In testimony before a congressional hearing in March 1876, the outspoken young officer had implicated some influential figures in a corruption scheme. The alleged crimes were kickbacks in the awarding of trading contracts for military posts in the West. The suspects, as implied by Custer's testimony, included Secretary of War William Belknap and Orvil Grant, the president's brother. Embarrassed by this testimony, the president suspended Custer from his command.

Custer begged to be reinstated. He went to the White House on three occasions, but the president refused to meet with him. Custer was allowed to return to duty only after generals Sherman, Sheridan, and Alfred H. Terry persuaded the president to relent. The officers argued that the campaign needed an experienced "Indian fighter." When Grant did, however, Custer was assigned to command a smaller unit within the Department of Dakota—the 7th Cavalry regiment—rather than the division itself. The overall field leadership of the Dakota column was assigned to General Terry, a former lawyer and Civil War veteran who had no experience in Native American warfare.

On May 17, 1876, the Dakota column departed Fort Abraham Lincoln on the Missouri River, bound west for the Powder River in Montana. The unit consisted of the 12 companies of Custer's mounted regiment, 5 companies of infantry or ground forces, 3 rapid-fire artillery pieces known as Gatling guns, 39 Native American scouts, more than 150 wagons, and 200 teamsters or wagon drivers. Obviously, such a large column moved very slowly, averaging fewer than 12 miles per day during the first two weeks.

By June 8, 1876, General Terry reached the Powder River with an advance party of the column, united with Colonel

Gibbons's division, and took command of both columns. Terry learned that the main camps of the Sioux and Northern Cheyennes were moving south along the Rosebud Creek toward General Crook's column. Nine days later, Crook's northward advance was halted by the surprise attack at Rosebud Creek.

While General Crook's column was involved in the Rosebud campaign, General Terry's command continued to search for the Native American camps. It proceeded along the southern bank of the Yellowstone River. Terry sent out a scouting unit under the command of Major Marcus A. Reno, which explored the area of the Tongue River and Rosebud Creek. The party learned that the Sioux and Northern Cheyennes were moving southward up the Rosebud. It appeared likely that they would cross over to the Little Bighorn River.

On June 19, 1876, Major Reno's unit rejoined General Terry's column near the Tongue River. Two days later, Terry presented a battle plan to his commanders. The overall goal was to engage the largest possible concentration of "hostiles" in warfare and to use the 7th Cavalry regiment as a mobile strike force. Custer's regiment would approach the Little Bighorn valley from the south. The remainder of Terry's command, including the infantry and Colonel Gibbons's 2nd Cavalry regiment, would then establish a blocking position. This unit would approach Little Bighorn from the north to prevent any escape of enemy warriors in that direction.

General Terry's written order to Colonel Custer instructed him to take an indirect route to the Little Bighorn. This was to allow time for the rest of the command to establish its blocking position. Custer was also ordered to take action to prevent any escape around his left flank to the south or southeast. Otherwise, General Terry gave Custer the freedom to follow his own instincts: "The Department Commander places too much confidence in your zeal, energy, and ability to wish to impose upon you precise orders which might hamper your action when nearly in contact with the enemy."[1]

Custer's strike force included all 12 companies of his regiment. It also included Arikara, Crow, and Sioux scouts and 175 pack mules carrying sufficient supplies for 15 days. Custer intended to travel light and as quickly as possible. He turned down General Terry's offer to bring the three Gatling guns, because they would slow down his movement. Military historians have speculated whether this decision was a mistake. If the Gatling guns had made it to the battlefield, they might have provided enough firepower to allow Custer's companies to survive on Last Stand Hill. Custer also refused Major James Brisbin's offer to include his 2nd Cavalry Regiment in the strike force. He told General Terry, "The 7th can handle anything it meets."[2]

Custer's Offensive

AN OFFICER OF AT LEAST THE RANK OF FIRST LIEUTENANT
commanded each of the 12 companies in Custer's regiment. Many of the commanders were extremely competent, but tension and petty bickering among the officers troubled the overall leadership of the regiment. Major Marcus Reno was second in command. Although he was an honored veteran of the Civil War, this was his first campaign involving Native American warfare. He was not well regarded by the other officers, and he and Custer did not trust one another. Custer also resented being placed in command of the regiment.

A letter of the alphabet designated each of the 12 companies, such as Company A. Captain Frederick Benteen was the leader of Company H in addition to being third in command as the senior company commander. He had served with distinction as a cavalry commander during the Civil War, and unlike Major Reno, he was an experienced veteran of Native American conflicts. He had served with Custer at the Battle of the Washita and had often criticized Custer's actions in that attack. Benteen's no-nonsense attitude about military affairs often placed him at odds with Custer's leadership style.

Two of Custer's relatives also served as company commanders. His younger brother, Captain Thomas W. Custer, led Company C. First Lieutenant James Calhoun, commander of Company L, was Custer's brother-in-law. In addition, another younger brother, Boston Custer, and Colonel Custer's 18-year-old nephew, Henry Armstrong Reed, accompanied the regiment as civilians with the supply train.

The troops of the 7th Cavalry were each armed with two standard weapons, a rifle and a pistol. The rifle was a .45/55-caliber Springfield Carbine and the pistol was a .45-caliber Colt revolver. (*Caliber* refers to the size of the bullets or ammunition a weapon fires.) Although both weapons were

MAJOR MARCUS ALBERT RENO: A SUBJECT OF CONTROVERSY

Marcus Reno (1834–1889) led the U.S. 7th Cavalry's first attack at Little Bighorn and wound up being the officer in charge of the only unit that survived the battle. Born in Carrolton, Illinois, he graduated from the U.S. Military Academy and was commissioned as a U.S. Army lieutenant in 1857. He was given the temporary rank of brigadier general for his meritorious service during the Civil War, but had a very troubled and controversial military career thereafter. Charged with cowardice and drunkenness for his actions at Little Bighorn, he was not punished by a court of inquiry in 1879. However, in 1877, his pay was suspended for two years for making advances on the wife of another officer. In 1880, he was discharged for drunkenness and assaulting a junior officer. In the 1960s, the U.S. Army declared the dismissal improper and permitted Reno's remains to be reburied with honors at the Little Bighorn cemetery.

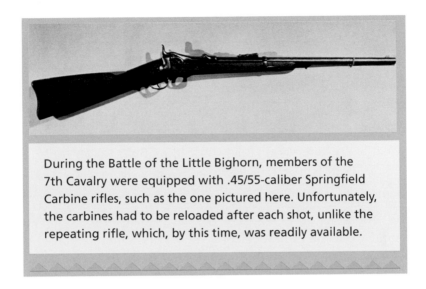

During the Battle of the Little Bighorn, members of the 7th Cavalry were equipped with .45/55-caliber Springfield Carbine rifles, such as the one pictured here. Unfortunately, the carbines had to be reloaded after each shot, unlike the repeating rifle, which, by this time, was readily available.

models developed in 1873, they did not represent the latest in firearm technology. The Springfield, for example, had to be reloaded after a single shot, while repeating rifles with twice its firing speed were widely available.

Many of the officers and most of the civilians brought along their own weapons. For example, Custer himself carried a Remington sporting rifle and two snub-nosed Irish pistols. Although each soldier was also issued a sword or saber, Custer ordered these weapons to be boxed before the strike force departed. The 7th Cavalry thus took the field without their infamous "Long Knives," the feature for which the soldiers were best known to the Sioux. The lack of swords would prove to be a disadvantage during some of the close fighting that lay ahead. However, their inclusion would not have changed the ultimate outcome.

On June 22, 1876, the regiment set out on its mission, following Rosebud Creek to the south. After breaking camp at 5:00 A.M. on the second day, the Native American scouts were sent ahead to explore the terrain. They discovered a southward trail made by Sioux ponies and evidence of campsites. The column followed this trail. On the third day, it came upon the Sun

Dance site where Sitting Bull had experienced his vision several weeks before. Later that afternoon, the regiment discovered a fresh trail that turned up Davis Creek in the direction of the valley of the Little Bighorn River. Custer believed that this meant they were very close to the main encampment. What he did not realize is that this new trail was made by bands that fled the Great Sioux Reservation following Sitting Bull's earlier trail.

On June 19, 1876, at their encampment near the Little Bighorn River, the main body of Sioux and Northern Cheyennes began a six-day celebration of the Battle of the Rosebud. By the end of that celebration, a mass influx of summer roamers from the reservation doubled the size of the camp. The village now contained perhaps 1,000 lodges and as many as 7,000 tribal members.

At sunset on June 24, the Native American scouts with the 7th Cavalry discovered further evidence of the presence of the Sioux and Northern Cheyennes in the Little Bighorn valley. They scanned the horizon from a lookout point called Crow's Nest, atop the summit of the divide between the Rosebud and Little Bighorn valleys. From that height, they noted that the trail they had been following continued past the divide. They also observed a few tepees about eight miles away down Reno Creek.

Upon learning this information, Custer decided to follow the trail despite his orders from General Terry to proceed southward. His plan was to conduct a night movement toward the Little Bighorn encampment, with the hope of a possible attack at dawn. Accordingly, the regiment began a night march up Davis Creek at 11:00 P.M. After proceeding about six miles in three hours, Custer ordered the command to halt and rest in preparation for battle. The tired men of the command had covered about 76 miles in three days.

When dawn broke on June 25, 1876, the Native American scouts reported new information to Second Lieutenant Charles A. Varnum, the officer in charge of the scouts. From

Crow's Nest, they saw smoke and a large herd of ponies about 15 miles to the northwest. This indicated a large encampment. Lieutenant Varnum went to Crow's Nest to confirm the observation, but only saw two tepees through his field glasses. Custer saw nothing when he later decided to personally scan the horizon from Crow's Nest.

Custer doubted the scout's earlier sighting. The only hard evidence he acknowledged of an encampment ahead was that indicated by the trail the regiment was following. The pony and travois tracks told them that there were several allied groups traveling with their families. A travois was a frame used by Native Americans to drag loads over land. Most often dragged by horses, the basic construction consisted of two long poles lashed together in the shape of an elongated isosceles triangle. The dragged poles made a distinct trail.

Custer viewed the presence of family members as a military advantage. He thought it would make the warriors more vulnerable and slow down any pursuit or escape. The Crow scouts told him that the number of Native American warriors ahead was greater than the number of cartridges in the regiment's ammunition supply. But their warnings had no effect on Custer; he was more concerned with preventing the Native American enemy's escape than he was with the actual size of the encampment.

While at Crow's Nest, Custer's brother Tom advised the commander that two Sioux parties had spotted the column. The Crow scouts warned that it would now be impossible to surprise the encampment. Custer disagreed with their assessment. He told two junior officers that he doubted that the encampment was in the Little Bighorn valley at all. Yet, when he later met with all of the officers, he reportedly told them that "the largest Indian camp on the North American Continent Is ahead." Custer may not have been convinced that this was true, but within a few hours his command found out that the scouting parties were right.

Custer gathered his officers after learning that another party of Sioux had sighted the regiment. He was now convinced that the element of surprise was lost. He told his troops that an immediate attack of the encampment was necessary to prevent escape. His plan was to divide the regiment into four groups and to proceed to the target area in three columns.

Captain Benteen was placed in charge of the first group, a battalion consisting of companies D, H, and K (120 men). Major Reno headed a second battalion made up of 175 men in companies A, G, and M. Custer took command of a third battalion of 221 men organized into two wings. Captain George W. Yates led a wing consisting of companies E and F. Captain Myles W. Keogh headed a wing made up of companies C, I, and L. The scouts under Lieutenant Varnum were to move ahead of the main column. The pack train, or supply unit, which included Company B, was to follow the main column.

Major Reno's battalion was to lead the main approach, with the Custer battalion to the right and the Benteen battalion to the left. Benteen was ordered to scout and cover the left flank of the approach; however, his route to the target area carried his battalion over a series of ridges that blocked any view of the main advance group. Benteen had objected to Custer's plan to divide the command. "Hadn't we better keep the regiment together?" he suggested. "If this is as big a camp as they say, we'll need every man we have."[4] Custer dismissed Benteen's worries. He had been successful at the Battle of the Washita in 1867 by dividing his command and attacking from different approaches. The difference then was he knew exactly where the target area was in that conflict. In the case of Little Bighorn, he lacked such critical knowledge when he ordered Captain Benteen to proceed on the left.

About 90 minutes after the command began its split approach up Reno Creek, the main body came upon the "lone tepee" spotted earlier from Crow's Nest. Sitting Bull's group

A native of Ireland, Myles Walter Keogh immigrated to the United States in 1862 and served under George Armstrong Custer at Little Bighorn. Although Keogh was killed during the battle, many Native American combatants claimed that he was one of the last members of his company to fall.

had encamped at that site nine days before. From that point, Custer observed a moving band of about 100 Native Americans a few miles ahead. They were Northern Cheyenne families traveling to join the main Sioux gathering, which was perhaps five miles ahead. Custer ordered an immediate pursuit of this band. He gave the following instructions to Major Reno, head of the lead battalion: "The Indians are about two miles and a half ahead. They are on the jump. Go forward as fast as you think proper, and charge them wherever you find them, and I will support you."[5]

Not having received any report of a main encampment, Custer may have thought that he would be up against several scattered smaller bands similar to the one the command was now chasing. If so, he could be fairly confident that any one of his battalions had the strength to defeat them. He ordered his Arikara scouts to advance and capture or set free the band's ponies. This was a favorite tactic of the cavalry, designed to limit the mobility of opposing forces. The Arikara scouts were reluctant to carry out this mission, though, because they still believed there was a major encampment ahead.

Warriors from the Northern Cheyenne band taunted the pursuing troops. By the time Major Reno's battalion reached the Little Bighorn River, the band had disappeared into a nearby wooded area. Reno's men crossed the Little Bighorn River at the mouth of Reno Creek and saw a portion of an active village about three miles ahead.

Although Custer had assured Reno that his battalion would follow in support, it did not do so. Instead, Custer ordered his men to veer toward the north, perhaps to attack farther downriver. The Little Bighorn flows from south to north). Evidently, Custer never communicated this change in tactics to Major Reno. Custer's five companies ascended high bluffs along the east bank of the Little Bighorn and proceeded northward.

ATTACK ON THE VILLAGE

As the valley ahead widened and the village became visible, Major Reno ordered his troops to move from a trot to a gallop. The charge was on. The soldiers saw before them great swirls of dust and smoke as villagers tried to drive ponies away and set grass fires to disguise their retreat. As the soldiers continued their gallop toward the village, it appeared they had the field to themselves, since no warriors challenged their approach. Full of adrenaline and emotion in the face of battle, they cheered wildly. Major Reno ordered the noise to stop. On the bluffs across the river, Custer witnessed Reno's charge. He expressed his happiness that the attack had surprised the village and that the Sioux and Northern Cheyennes were fleeing.

Reno's charge was a surprise to Sitting Bull's village even though isolated tribal members who had observed Custer's approaching column earlier in the day had brought back warnings. However, their reports were not received in time to prepare for Reno's attack.

The unsuspecting villagers were engaged in routine daily tasks. Some of the Hunkpapa women, such as Pretty White Buffalo and Moving Robe, were digging wild prairie turnips. Antelope, a Northern Cheyenne woman also known as Kate Bighead, was bathing in the river with some Minneconjou friends. Thirteen-year-old Black Elk, who later became an important Oglala holy man, was also swimming in the stream. Other tribal members were fishing or playing along the river. Low Dog, an Oglala, was napping in his lodge. White Bull, a Minneconjou and nephew of Sitting Bull, was herding his horses. Another Minneconjou named Standing Bear was eating in a tepee with his uncle and elderly, weak grandmother. Some of the women were taking down their tepees in preparation for eventually moving the village downriver.

Those who saw the approaching soldiers spread an alarm. Criers ran through the village warning all of its residents. Chaos spread throughout the camp. Warriors rushed to grab their weapons and ponies. Some women and children screamed and cried in fear. Elders shouted advice. The Hunkpapa warrior Gall remembered that an order was given to strike the camp. Yet many people fled to the west without their tepees or belongings. Once mounted, a few warriors galloped to meet Reno's charge. They hoped to delay the attack long enough to allow the women and children to escape. "Boys, take courage," Sitting Bull coached them. "Would you see these little children be taken away from me as dogs?"[6]

It was the usual Sioux custom to scatter and flee from attack if possible. Gall later reported that Reno's approach came too quickly to allow an escape. Custer's greatest fear in approaching the battle was that the tribes might actually succeed in running away.

Then, an odd event took place that changed the momentum of the entire battle. The village lay almost defenseless before Reno. His battalion had not made contact with any opposition or suffered a casualty. Yet, the major suddenly halted the charge about a quarter mile from the village.

ANTELOPE (KATE BIGHEAD): EYEWITNESS TO LITTLE BIGHORN

Antelope was a Cheyenne woman who witnessed much of the Little Bighorn battle while searching for her nephew Noisy Walking. Born a Southern Cheyenne, her family became associated with the Northern Cheyennes and lived with them in the Black Hills country, when not traveling with Crazy Horse's Oglalas. Her older brother Ice (White Bull) was a leading Cheyenne holy man in Sitting Bull's village. His only son, Noisy Walking, an 18-year-old warrior, rode off with the "suicide boys" soon after spotting soldiers across the river. As a refugee from the Washita battle of 1867, Antelope was familiar with Custer and claimed he fathered a child by her cousin. She therefore recognized him when she witnessed other Cheyenne women pushing awls into the ears of his corpse. After a two-hour search, Antelope finally found Noisy Walking lying in the Deep Ravine and badly wounded. He died later that evening.

Instead of continuing into the camp, as ordered, Reno directed his battalion to dismount and form a skirmish line.

The reason for this order has never been explained satisfactorily. Reno later said that he saw a ditch ahead full of hundreds of warriors waiting in ambush. However, such a defensive position was never confirmed, either by other soldiers of his battalion or by defenders of the village. Reno had no experience in Native American warfare and did not know the position of his support battalions, including Custer's companies. Seeing that the village was not in full flight and that warriors were rushing out to meet his charge, he likely decided that a mounted attack could not succeed.

Many historians and military strategists maintain that Reno's decision was the first fatal flaw in the U.S. Army's attack. If his battalion had continued its mounted charge into the village, they argue, it might have driven the warriors into the waiting arms of Custer's five companies. If Captain Benteen's battalion could have arrived in time to support Custer in this scenario, the outcome of the battle might have been more favorable for the U.S. Army.

But, in defense of Reno's decision, he did not know Custer's position when the attack began. The evidence makes it clear that Reno's understanding of the battle plan was that Custer's troops would support his battalion from the rear.

Upon dismounting, every fourth man in Reno's battalion led the horses to the rear. The others formed a skirmish line of fewer than 100 men and began firing their carbines toward the village. These shots ripped through the tepees and killed as many as 10 women and children.

Success of the Counterattack

MAJOR RENO'S TROOPERS HAD ASSAULTED THE SOUTHERN end of the village where the Hunkpapas were lodged. This was Sitting Bull's camp and, in effect, the headquarters of the resistance leaders. The Hunkpapas were therefore the first responders to the attack. They were the first warriors to gallop toward the skirmish line, while most of the women, children, and elders fled the camp. Boys guarding the pony herd outside the village drove the horses toward the camp so that they would be accessible to the warriors.

Sitting Bull, the 45-year-old leader of the village, did not join the battle. Recovering from a recent gunshot wound to his foot, he determined that he could play a more important role by looking after the safety of the families and encouraging the young warriors. Sitting Bull gave his war club and shield to One Bull, his Minneconjou nephew, and instructed him to attempt to negotiate with the attackers. "Parley with them, if you can," advised the Hunkpapa medicine man. "If they are willing, tell them I will talk peace with them."[7]

One Bull soon discovered that the gunfire of the attackers was too intense to carry out his mission. Sitting Bull also changed his mind about the possibility of peace talks after one of his horses was shot in two places. "Now my best horse is shot," he declared. "It is like they have shot me. Attack them."[8]

One Bull then joined the warriors in the initial counterattack. Young Black Moon, Swift Bear, White Bull, and Good Bear Boy rode with him. Young warriors, hoping to count coup, rode close to Reno's skirmish line, daring the soldiers to fire on them. As more mounted warriors reached the scene, they tried to flank, or encircle, Reno's line.

Private George M. Smith of Company M was probably the first soldier to die in the battle. His frantic horse bolted and carried him into the charging line of warriors.

The old Hunkpapa chief Black Moon brought up a party of village police. They drove off the Arikara scouts and went around Reno's line on the left. At about the same time, One Bull led a charge directly into the line, causing the soldiers to scramble. After the warriors circled back to regroup, One Bull noticed that Good Bear Boy had fallen. He lay on the ground about 30 yards from Reno's line. One Bull raced back to the battlefield to rescue him. Amid heavy fire, One Bull hoisted the young warrior onto his pony. He managed to bring him to safety, even though his pony was wounded in its hind leg.

The soldiers increased their fire in spite of the fact that most warriors were out of range. They quickly exhausted their ammunition supply and had to take turns retreating to their horses to get further ammo from their saddlebags. This weakened the attack. No effort was made to control the heavy rate of gunfire. The fact that the villagers suffered relatively few casualties during Reno's attack reflected the poor weapons training and discipline of the 7th Cavalry.

In the meantime, Custer's battalion continued to ride northward. The steep bluffs along the Little Bighorn concealed their movement, but also blocked their view of the valley. The commander received a report that the warriors were not fleeing but were instead riding out to fight Reno's men. Upon ascending bluffs near Wier Point, Custer got his first full view of the enormous size of the village he was attempting to capture. He observed hundreds of families fleeing to the north. He also witnessed hundreds of warriors moving toward Major Reno's skirmish line. This was Custer's last view of the Reno battalion.

Custer knew upon overlooking the battle in the valley that he needed additional support to continue any offensive assault. He sent a message to Captain Benteen, who was following somewhere to the rear, to have his battalion and the pack train quickly join him. There were problems with the communication, though. The soldier whom Custer chose to deliver the message was Private John Martin, a trumpeter and orderly in Company H. Martin was an Italian immigrant, whose original name was Giovanni Martini. Because he spoke little English, a junior officer wrote the message on notepaper. First Lieutenant William W. Cooke was a Canadian soldier of fortune who joined the U.S. Army during the Civil War. He hastily scribbled the following message: "Benteen. Come On. Big Village. Be Quick. Bring Packs. W.W. Cooke, P.[S.] bring packs."[9]

There was no reason why Custer could not have chosen a messenger more fluent in English to deliver the information verbally. There was also no reason why the note could not have better described Custer's situation with more specific information. For example, the postscript was probably intended to read, "bring ammunition packs," but the key word was left out.

Private Martin managed to deliver the note to Benteen within a half hour, although his horse suffered a bullet

During the Battle of the Little Bighorn, Captain Frederick Benteen was the leader of Company H of the 7th Cavalry and third in command behind George Armstrong Custer and Marcus Reno. Despite being wounded during the battle, Benteen played a large role in holding off the Sioux after Custer's battalion had been annihilated.

wound. The captain, however, trailed too far behind to be able to "Be Quick" in responding. He ordered his battalion to ride ahead at a trot, but decided not to wait for the pack train. Some scholars maintain that if Benteen would have

"Come On" immediately with all the men and supplies, he might have reached the battle in time to help Custer's battalion. He did not, though. As it turned out, Private Martin became the last soldier who saw Custer alive and lived to talk about it.

Captain Benteen may have gotten the wrong impression of the situation from Private Martin's verbal descriptions. Benteen and some of his men understood Martin to say that Major Reno's battalion had attacked the village and was killing all of the villagers. This, of course, was not the case. Custer and his battalion resumed their ride northward (downstream). He was likely looking for a break in the bluffs that would allow him to descend into the village to join the battle.

MAJOR RENO'S RETREAT

Meanwhile, down in the valley, the counterattacking Sioux and Northern Cheyenne warriors were continuing to flank Reno's skirmish line. Afraid of being surrounded, the battalion retreated to a stand of timber. It remains unclear whether this retreat was ordered by Reno or if the men decided to move on their own. Private Theodore Goldin described their situation: "We were forced to face about and endeavor to repel their advances until we could get our horses into the timber. . . . Soon after this we retired into the timber, where we had better protection, and resumed the fight."[10]

The battalion retreated without any tactical covering fire. The sudden movement of the soldiers and drop in gunfire prompted some Sioux warriors to believe that the battle was over. The Oglala leader Crazy Horse and his warriors arrived on the scene at this time. His Oglala comrade Short Bull, a nephew of the famous leader Red Cloud, yelled to him that they had missed the fight. As a result, Crazy Horse held his warriors back for a while.

After the Battle of the Little Bighorn, many U.S. Army officials and the general public looked for a scapegoat to help explain how a unit of Native Americans could defeat the U.S. Army. The blame largely fell on Major Marcus A. Reno (pictured here), but he was cleared of any wrongdoing by a court of inquiry in 1879.

When Reno's men retreated, so, too, did the Arikara scouts who had tried to drive away the village's ponies. They'd had little success, but killed at least six women during their effort. Reno's men found protection in the dense stand of timber, which offered them a good site from which to defend themselves. They might have been able to hold this position for hours, keeping the attacking warriors at bay until the other battalions arrived. But the increasing pressure of the warriors' counterattack caused Reno to panic after just 20 minutes.

The warriors completely surrounded Reno's position and began to enter the woods at various points. Most warriors fought as individuals, but One Bull, Two Moon, Hawk Man, Old Black Moon, and others also led war parties into the fray. It was Crazy Horse, however, riding his white-faced pony, who inspired the most convincing charge into the timber.

Major Reno decided at this point that the high bluffs across the Little Bighorn to the east offered a better defensive position. The problem with this plan was that physical obstacles made it impossible to get his men to the bluffs safely. First, there was a mile and a half of open ground between the woods and the river. Then there was the river water itself to ford, an 8-foot-high bank on the other side, and 100-foot bluffs to climb.

Major Reno decided to make his move without ordering a bugle call that would have alerted his entire unit. Some of his junior officers heard his verbal orders, but others did not. Reno gave no thought to posting soldiers to provide cover for the movement. As a result, warriors were able to sneak through the underbrush and fire on the unit at close range. Bloody Knife, Custer's favorite Arikara scout, was shot in the head as he mounted a horse next to Reno. His blood splattered over Reno's face and uniform.

Reno panicked and issued a series of contradicting orders. He told his men to dismount, and then quickly ordered them

back on their horses. Some troops misunderstood the commands and others had no idea what action was to be carried
out. Major Reno lost his hat in the confusion and decided to
tie a red bandana around his head. Appearing like a crazed
man, he bolted ahead of the defensive line and yelled: "Any of
you men who wish to live, make your escape—follow me."[11]

Most of the disorganized battalion followed their leader
into the clearing. The Northern Cheyenne Wooden Leg recalled that upon observing this movement, the warriors
thought the soldiers were attacking. Then they realized, to
their surprise, that they were trying to flee. The warriors responded by riding within about 50 feet of the flanks of the
scattered retreat formation and opened fire.

The warriors' attack was a classic example of their most
successful tactic in both warfare and hunting. It has often
been likened to a buffalo hunt. The warriors quickly rode up
on fresh ponies and attacked the exposed troopers one by
one at close range. They shot or clubbed the soldiers out of
their saddles. The soldiers also made themselves easy targets
as they struggled in the water while trying to cross the Little
Bighorn and trying to climb the bluffs on the other side. One
unit mistakenly climbed a bluff occupied by warriors at the
top. These soldiers were shot and scalped in full view of their
other fleeing comrades.

Isaiah Dorman, a civilian interpreter, was among those
killed during the retreat. Known to the Sioux as *wascimum sapa*, "the black white man," he was the only African
American to serve with Custer's regiment. Dorman, who was
probably a runaway slave from Alabama or Louisiana, was
married to a Santee woman. Having learned Sioux dialects
as a result of living among one of the bands, he periodically
served the U.S. Army as an interpreter. As a mounted warrior
caught up with Dorman during the retreat, Dorman turned
and shot him through the heart. This drew the attention of
other warriors who fired several shots into Dorman's horse.

The animal fell over on its back, trapping Dorman underneath it. A Hunkpapa woman coming upon this scene killed Dorman with a rifle shot to the head. This woman may have been Moving Robe, the 23-year-old daughter of the warrior Crawler. She was seeking revenge for the death of her younger brother Deeds, whom the Arikara scouts killed in the earliest stage of Reno's attack.

Soldiers were later horrified when they discovered Dorman's corpse. The body was more brutally mutilated than was usually the case among victims of Sioux warfare. It appeared that Dorman was singled out for special attention, so that he would not make a good appearance in the spirit world. His pierced, skinned, and severed remains were meant to stand as a symbol of what was viewed as his betrayal of the Sioux.

Those of Reno's command who made it across the Little Bighorn straggled to the top of a bluff, which became known as Reno Hill. The major was reportedly the first to arrive. An hour into Reno's attack, his 175-man command had lost 40 men, including three officers. Most had been killed during the dash from the timber. Thirteen wounded men made it to the top of the bluff, but 37 soldiers remained missing. Seventeen of these soldiers were left in the woods during the retreat, but managed to reunite with the battalion later.

The casualties were not one-sided. The warriors lost perhaps eight of their party, including two brothers of the Hunkpapa bandleader Crow King. However, the kill ratio at that point was five to one in favor of the Native Americans.

Doctor Henry R. Porter was the acting assistant surgeon with Reno's battalion. He had graduated from the Georgetown University School of Medicine four years before. After attending to the wounded on the bluff, Porter advised Major Reno that the soldiers were quite demoralized by the disastrous retreat. Annoyed by this statement, Reno replied, "That was a cavalry charge, sir!"[12]

Frederick F. Gerard was one of the men left stranded in the timber. A French-American fluent in Arikara and Sioux dialects, he served the battalion as a civilian interpreter and scout. Gerard had quite a different opinion of Reno's

Pictured here in the 1880s, Curley, or Ashishishe, enlisted in the U.S. Army as an Indian scout in April 1876. A member of the Crow tribe, Curley served under Custer at the Battle of the Little Bighorn, and his account of the conflict was later translated and reprinted in many newspapers.

LITTLE-KNOWN COMBATANTS AT LITTLE BIGHORN

Private John Martin (1853–1922) was the messenger who carried Lieutenant Cooke's "Be Quick" message to Captain Benteen. He thus became the last survivor of the regiment to see Custer alive. Born Giovanni Martini in Sola Consalina, Italy, Martin immigrated to the United States in 1873 and enlisted in the U.S. Army in 1874. Serving as an orderly and trumpeter, he retired as a sergeant in 1904. He then worked as a subway ticket agent in New York until his death.

Isaiah Dorman (c. 1821–1876) was the only known person of African-American ancestry to die in the Little Bighorn battle. Likely a runaway slave from the D'Orman family of Louisiana and Alabama, he married a Santee Sioux woman and fathered two sons. Employed to serve as a guide for the U.S. 7th Cavalry, he was tortured and killed during Reno's retreat. Native American accounts claim that he was singled out for extreme mutilation for betraying the Sioux.

Moving Robe (Tashna Mani) (c. 1854–1940) was one of the few Sioux women to fight at Little Bighorn and a likely accomplice in Isaiah Dorman's death. Her younger brother Deeds was killed in Reno's initial attack. Seeking revenge, the 23-year-old rode with her Hunkpapa father in the counterattack against Reno. The Oglala warrior Eagle Elk said it was Moving Robe who fired the fatal shot into the badly wounded Dorman as he sat begging for his life.

Minton "Mitch" Bouyer (Boyer) (1837–1876) was the interpreter and scout who advised Custer that he faced more warriors than his command could handle. Despite his misgivings, he remained at Custer's side, becoming the only scout to die with him on Last Stand Hill. The son of a French trapper and a Santee Sioux woman, Bouyer was fluent in English, Lakota, and Crow. Bone fragments discovered on the battlefield in 1987 were identified as his remains.

movement. The Native Americans "picked off the troops at will," he said, "It was a rout, not a charge!"[13]

The troops on Reno Hill were too preoccupied with their survival to notice that the counterattacking warriors had broken off contact. Only a few shooters remained to harass Reno's frazzled force, which no longer threatened the village. The vast majority of the warriors shifted focus and rode north to confront another pressing threat.

After observing Major Reno's battle in the valley, Custer decided to continue his offensive movement northward along the ridge east of the river, and to look for a place to cross the Little Bighorn. His battalion reached the Medicine Lodge Coulee at about 3:45 P.M. (A coulee is a river tributary that only flows seasonally.) This was the first location where the river might be forded to gain entry into the Native American village. About 15 minutes after arriving at this point, scouts Mitch Bouyer and Curley reached Custer with the news of Reno's retreat.

Custer listened to their report and then dismissed them. He told them that they had accomplished their mission of guiding him to the village and should return to the pack train. Bouyer—the mixed-blood Sioux scout whose unheeded warnings to Custer of a larger village than expected had now become reality—stubbornly chose to ride on with the battalion. Consequently, he became the only Native American scout to die with Custer's unit. Curley, a Crow tribal member, headed eastward. He disguised himself in the blanket of a dead Sioux warrior and watched Custer's defeat from more than a mile away.

Custer Rides the Ridges

CUSTER THEN MOVED HIS COMMAND TO A RIDGE ABOVE the coulee to observe and assess the combat situation. It was there that his battalion was first observed by both Native American warriors and women who had ascended the bluffs across the river. The discovery of additional troops came as a shock. The Two Kettle warrior Runs the Enemy recalled that it looked as if thousands of bluecoat soldiers filled the ridge. These soldiers posed the threat of positioning themselves between the warriors and the village.

Those who saw them quickly spread an alarm. The battle then shifted from the valley to the hills. Other warriors, including One Bull, Fears Nothing, and Red Feather had also observed the arrival of some of Captain Benteen's companies at Reno's position on the bluffs. This likewise came as a surprise.

From his vantage point on the ridge, Custer observed the Native Americans on the bluffs who saw his battalion for the first time. He may have also seen the approach of Captain Benteen's units. The apparent strategy he developed was to advance part of his command down a ridge toward a ford to the village (Deep Coulee Ford) to draw pressure away from Major Reno's struggling battalion. (A ford is a place in a river that is shallow enough to permit a crossing of the stream.) The rest of his men would proceed to some advantageous position farther north. They could then turn westward to confront the warriors. The combined Reno and Benteen units might then follow the warriors drawn toward Custer's advance unit moving toward the ford. If the strategy worked, the warriors would be trapped between the two commands.

Custer thus dispatched the left wing of his battalion down Nye-Cartwright Ridge, along Butler Ridge, and toward the ford to the village. This wing consisted of companies E and F (about 80 troops). Captain Yates commanded that wing, in addition to commanding Company F. Yates had served with Custer since the Civil War. First Lieutenant Algernon E. Smith, another Civil War veteran, led Company E. This company was known as the "Gray Horse Troop," because they rode light-colored mounts.

Captain Yates had no intension of crossing the Little Bighorn into the camp. The northern part of the village was by then almost empty and most of the families had fled to the northeast. They sought refuge in an area of streams and bluffs known as Squaw Creek. (*Squaw* is a derogatory term for Native American women, but this area still officially retains that name.) The majority of the warriors were either still at the site of the Reno battle or returning from it. The Yates wing descended from Nye-Cartwright Ridge. As the Gray Horse Troop approached the ford, it initially faced only a handful of Northern Cheyenne warriors, including Bobtail Horse, Roan Bear, and Buffalo Calf. Most of the Native Americans who witnessed the early exchange of fire recalled that these men forded the Little Bighorn and confronted the soldiers east of the river. They were soon joined by a large group of other warriors who raced from Reno Hill to face

Captain George W. Yates, who had served with Custer since the Civil War and was one of his good friends, commanded companies E and F of the 7th Cavalry during the Battle of the Little Bighorn. Like Custer, Yates was killed during the battle.

the new threat. Soldiers and warriors shot at each other with little impact.

After bullets began flying back and forth, the warrior Yellow Nose suddenly started racing his pony toward the soldiers' firing line, near the western end of Butler Ridge. Other tribesmen followed him. Yellow Nose was a member of the

Ute tribe of present-day Utah and had been adopted by the Northern Cheyennes. As he approached the soldiers, a color bearer for the U.S. troops carried the regimental guidon and rode toward him. The color bearer positioned his guidon like a spear and Yellow Nose met the challenge head-on. After the two fighters clashed, they jousted like a pair of medieval knights. Yellow Nose managed to seize the guidon, which he mistook for a rifle at first. With a shrill war whoop, he hoisted the flag high in the air so that other warriors would be spirited by his coup. The loss of the guidon was a psychological blow and bad omen for the cavalry. Yellow Nose's deed became one of the best-remembered stories of the battle that elders passed on to future generations.

The right wing of Custer's battalion remained on the ridge. Headed by Captain Keogh, it consisted of companies C, I, and L. Keogh was an Irish-born soldier of fortune. He had served with distinction in the Civil War and had been with the 7th Cavalry for almost 10 years.

More warriors made their presence known along the line between the East and Nye-Cartwright ridges. The Northern Cheyenne Wolf Tooth, his cousin Big Foot, and a party of 50 other warriors stumbled into Keogh's wing in a coulee near Luce Ridge. Wolf Tooth's party had not been in the village and had only recently been informed of Reno's attack while out riding east of the Little Bighorn. They decided to go back to the village by riding along the ridgeline. Soon discovering that there were soldiers between them and the village, they quickly devised a plan of attack. The party split up and half rode south to follow the troops up the ridgeline that extended to the northwest. The rest circled the soldiers to try to cut them off from the north.

The Wolf Tooth party began harassing the troops moving along the ridges. Once the soldiers of Keogh's wing started firing at them, however, most of the warriors backed off and moved to a higher position. Wolf Tooth and Big Foot followed the troops from afar, waiting for another opportunity to strike. Their statements after the battle have helped historians reconstruct the movements of Custer's battalion after it confronted their party. Wolf Tooth recalled that this short fight was the first skirmish of the battle in the hills. It actually took place roughly within the same 10-minute segment when Yellow Nose seized the Yates company guidon (between 4:20 and 4:30 P.M.). At about this same time, Captain Benteen's full battalion finally reached Major Reno's routed troops, who were huddled on Reno Hill. Upon seeing Benteen approach, the warriors still chasing Reno halted their offensive and withdrew toward the village.

Once Captain Yates's wing began to attract warriors on Butler Ridge, Keogh's troops fired their rifles in unison to signal the Yates wing to withdraw and return to the ridge. They must have also hoped that this volley would signal the now combined Reno and Benteen battalions to proceed to the sound of gunfire. But these soldiers remained on Reno Hill still awaiting the arrival of the pack train.

Colonel Custer observed the developments from the East Ridge. Just after Keogh's volley, he led the right wing northward to Nye-Cartwright Ridge. Captain Yates's wing then ascended Butler Ridge to reunite with the rest of the battalion on Nye-Cartwright. Although Yates's withdrawal was part of Custer's plan, the warriors thought they had turned the soldiers back, especially since the retreat took place just after Yellow Nose seized the guidon. Yates's probe got no closer to the Little Bighorn River than a quarter mile.

If it was Yates's mission to attract warriors to the battalion, the strategy succeeded. Many warriors raced eastward up Deep Coulee in pursuit of Yates's men. Keogh's three companies on the ridge had skirmished briefly with Wolf Tooth's party and Custer could see more warriors streaming up Deep Coulee from the west. If given enough time, these warriors posed the threat of encircling his soldiers on the north. Once his wings reunited on Nye-Cartwright Ridge,

First Lieutenant James Calhoun, Custer's brother-in-law, commanded Company L of the 7th Cavalry during the Battle of the Little Bighorn. Although most of the members of Company L were killed, including Calhoun, the unit was one of the few that showed organization during the battle.

Custer thus found it necessary to move northwest to Calhoun Hill, the next high ground. This hill formed the southern nose of Battle Ridge, a high ridge that extended north for about half a mile. Last Stand Hill formed the northern nose of Battle Ridge.

Custer moved his battalion to Calhoun Hill to keep the warriors between themselves and the Reno and Benteen battalions, who were still on the bluffs about four miles to the south. It also gave them a chance to wait for the arrival of these battalions. Custer's combined wings rode in double battle columns to Calhoun Hill. They arrived by 4:40 P.M. Upon arrival, Custer again divided his companies. Companies C, E, I, and L went into a holding action, executing a standard

FIRST LIEUTENANT JAMES CALHOUN: BROTHER-IN-LAW OF GEORGE ARMSTRONG CUSTER

James Calhoun (1845–1876) was the commander of the U.S. 7th Cavalry's Company L, which was crushed between two wings of Native American attackers on a hill that was later named in his memory. Born in Cincinnati, Ohio, he served as an enlisted infantryman during the latter years of the Civil War. He was commissioned as an infantry second lieutenant in 1867, and in 1870, he started dating Margaret Emma Custer, younger sister of George Armstrong Custer. The lieutenant colonel liked Calhoun and helped him get promoted and assigned to the 7th Cavalry in 1871, the year before James married "Maggie." He was nicknamed "Adonis" for his good looks, but the Custer family was concerned that he regularly gambled away money playing cards. Calhoun was a witness to Custer's signing of his last will and testament and served as his regimental adjutant during the 7th's Yellowstone and Black Hills expeditions.

formation from the U.S. Cavalry textbook. Company L, commanded by First Lieutenant James Calhoun, established a semicircular skirmish line on the southwest side of the hill. The other companies waited in reserve at positions on the reverse slope. Calhoun, Custer's brother-in-law, was later killed in action on this hill, which was named in his honor.

At this time, the skirmish line began firing on the approaching warriors. Meanwhile, Captain Yates's Company F, accompanied by Custer and his staff, continued northward along Battle Ridge. Warriors attempted to disrupt this movement, without success. The company rode about a mile beyond Custer Hill, observing the lay of the land for future maneuvers. They came within sight of a ford farther north along the Little Bighorn. Across the river they could also see hundreds of families that had escaped the village to find refuge in the Squaw Creek area. It must have become obvious to Custer at that point that he needed the Reno and Benteen battalions to join him before he could launch an offensive. The Native American families were a primary target in Custer's strategy. If they could be taken hostage, he told his subordinates, it would break the spirit of the warriors. But he would require all of his regiment to capture the families at Squaw Creek.

WARRIOR ENCROACHMENT

Warriors followed in the wake of Custer's movement to Calhoun Hill and encroached on his positions from three flanks. The majority of the warriors had crossed the river at Deep Coulee Ford and trailed up the ford to the ridges. They were mostly Lakota, including White Bull, the Minneconjou nephew of Sitting Bull. Another group of warriors, mostly Northern Cheyennes led by Lame White Man, worked its way north nearer to the eastern bank of the Little Bighorn. It kept a position between Custer and the village. This group had also crossed the river at the Deep Coulee Ford. A third group, including the Oglala warrior Crazy Horse, forded the river farther north of the village. It proceeded up Deep Ravine and crossed the Battle Ridge north of the Keogh-Calhoun wing. These warriors positioned themselves for an attack from the east.

When Lieutenant Calhoun's troops halted to form a skirmish line on Calhoun Hill, it gave the warriors an opportunity to organize. They crept toward the soldiers, often crawling low to the ground to remain hidden. They exposed themselves only long enough to fire rifles or shoot arrows. The Two Kettle known as Runs the Enemy observed "hundreds and hundreds" of warriors "in the coulees all around."[14] Antelope (Kate Bighead), a Northern Cheyenne woman who witnessed many of the battle scenes, recalled that "the fighting was slow and few were killed as both sides remained hidden."[15]

At about 4:50 P.M., a group of Sioux warriors decided to launch a mounted charge against the soldiers' skirmish line. The Minneconjous Hump and White Bull, the Oglala Red Feather, and Runs the Enemy were among this attacking war party. The charge met heavy fire from the deployed cavalrymen and was quickly driven back. Although the return fire dislodged many warriors from their horses, few were killed or wounded. Realizing that an open charge could not overcome the soldiers, the warriors circled back to consider another approach.

The warriors' attack was loud enough to be heard by the soldiers back on Reno Hill. Earlier they had heard heavy gunfire to the north. To some it sounded like volleys that might have been fired as a signal. The noise prompted Captain Thomas B. Weir to request Major Reno's permission to allow his Company D to proceed in the direction of the firing. Company D had previously been scouting with Captain Benteen's battalion.

Reno ordered Weir to remain in position, and the two argued. The captain had little faith in Reno's leadership. Weir had served with Custer for more than 10 years and was extremely loyal to him; therefore, he decided to defy Reno's order. With his company in tow, Weir advanced northward to a higher place now known as Weir Point. This point was about two miles south of Last Stand Hill. From that vantage point, Weir later witnessed Custer's final battle. If Reno and Benteen had shared Weir's instincts and decided to advance sooner, they might have saved the day for the 7th Cavalry. Instead, they waited for the pack train to arrive before they set out.

The failed Sioux charge against Company L's skirmish line on Calhoun Hill was followed by continued long-range firing and further encroachment of more warriors up the gullies. While Captain Keogh's companies were preoccupied with the firepower coming from the south and east, a group of warriors infiltrated Calhoun Hill from the west. This war party included many Hunkpapas who had been among the

TWO MOON (ISH HAYU NISHUS): NORTHERN CHEYENNE LEADER

Two Moon (1842–1917) was one of the prominent Northern Cheyenne war leaders at Little Bighorn. He was one of the nine chiefs of the Kit Fox Warrior society and a minor chief within the entire tribe. He was born in the Shoshone country of western Wyoming, the son of an Arikara captive who had married a Northern Cheyenne women. He led charges at the Little Bighorn against Reno's men in the timbers and the Gray Horse Troop on Battle Ridge. In April 1877, he surrendered his band to Colonel Nelson Miles at Fort Keogh, Montana. Thereafter, he remained at peace and supported Cheyenne progress in adapting to Euro-American culture. He spent his remaining years on the Northern Cheyenne Reservation in a log cabin near Rosebud Creek. He represented his tribe in Washington, D.C., on several occasions and met with President Woodrow Wilson in 1914.

last to leave the Reno fight. To meet this challenge, two platoons from Company C were ordered to move from east of Battle Ridge down to Finley Ridge near Calhoun Coulee.

At about 5:10 P.M., the Northern Cheyenne warrior Two Moon led a charge against the Gray Horse Troop of Company E. Lieutenant Smith's company had dismounted on the Battle Ridge near Last Stand Hill. Two Moon's warriors attacked from the west side of the ridge. The cavalrymen managed to deflect the charge with heavy return fire and the Cheyenne warriors withdrew to the east side of the ridge.

At about this same time, Custer and Captain Yates's Company F returned south to the Battle Ridge from their exploration of the north fork area. They halted where the Little Bighorn battle's cemetery is now located, which is sometimes called Cemetery Ridge. The five companies were now in line along the ridge, from Finley Ridge north to Cemetery Ridge. In order from south to north were companies C, L, I, E, and F. Still thinking offensively, Custer did not establish any defensive perimeter around the ridgeline. He was probably not aware that warriors were forming a U-shaped line around his battalion and that their number was increasing rapidly.

Warriors continued to make their way up Deep Ravine from the west. Company I, led by First Lieutenant James Porter, was deployed on the east side of Battle Ridge. Porter graduated from West Point after the Civil War and had no combat experience. His unit was dealing with the approach of Crazy Horse's group from the east and probably had no idea of the threat filtering up from the west.

The Battalion Disintegrates

DURING THIS STAGE OF THE BATTLE, SOME WARRIORS were successful in their goal of stampeding or capturing cavalry horses. A favorite war tactic of the Sioux and Northern Cheyennes was to separate an enemy from its horses, thereby crippling its mobility. Captured horses were also considered one of the key prizes of warfare. The loss of horses was a severe disadvantage to cavalry units, since they were trained primarily to be a mounted strike force. (It should be noted that the U.S. Cavalry also engaged in the practice of capturing Indian war ponies, but they often killed them.)

The horses of the men deployed along the ridge were led to the rear. U.S. soldiers assigned as horse holders kept them in place, usually four animals to a man. Warriors encroaching from the west waved blankets and shot arrows and bullets at the horses, causing some to break away. Wooden Leg recalled seeing horses pierced with arrows bucking about and knocking down their holders. Managing and protecting the horses became an increasingly critical problem for the soldiers.

Company E, the Gray Horse Troop, was ordered to move down from the area of the present Little Bighorn monument to the divide between Cemetery Ravine and Deep Ravine. Lieutenant Smith's task was to check the growing threat to the rear of Keogh's wing and clear out infiltrators in the Deep Ravine area.

Native Americans who witnessed the charge of the Gray Horse Troop, including Cheyenne tribal members Wooden Leg and Antelope, and Red Horse, a Minneconjou, recalled that the soldiers galloped down a gulch and the warriors fell back. Later, Red Horse drew a pictograph of the soldiers charging. For the moment, Company E held the advantage and succeeded in establishing a defensive perimeter, or battle line. But the warriors' retreat did not last long.

WHITE BULL (PTE-SAN-HUNKA): NEPHEW OF SITTING BULL

White Bull (1849–1947) was one of the most daring Sioux warriors at Little Bighorn. Born in South Dakota's Black Hills into a prominent family, his father was the Minneconjou chief Makes Room, and his uncle was Sitting Bull. Following the battle, he fled with his uncle's band to Canada, but became a victim of his old trick of counting coup on soldiers by riding in close. After being badly wounded in the arm, he surrendered in October 1876. Thereafter, he pursued assimilation into Euro-American society with the same vigor he displayed on the battlefield. Although named a chief of his tribe in 1881, he became a literate Congregationalist, a successful rancher, an agency policeman, and a tribal judge. He also husbanded 13 wives during his long life. At the 50th anniversary celebration of Little Bighorn in 1926, White Bull led the procession of surviving participants.

During the Battle of the Little Bighorn, White Bull, Sitting Bull's nephew, counted 7 coups, killed 2 soldiers, and captured 12 horses. Pictured here in 1890, White Bull would lead the procession of surviving participants during the 50th anniversary of the battle in 1926.

Meanwhile, on the southeast side of Battle Ridge, the soldiers and warriors seemed to have reached a stalemate. Bored with the lack of action, White Bull decided to stir things up by making a solo run toward Company I's skirmish line. Whipping up his pony to full speed, he headed directly toward a gap between a line of soldiers. He rode bareback without a rein, leaning low on his mount and holding on to his pony's neck. Rifles cracked all down the line as White Bull made a center run. He dashed right through the line and rode around half of the troops. Then he broke through another gap near the end of the line and headed back to his astonished friends on the warriors' line. Riding up to Crazy Horse, White Bull shouted, "Hokahey, brother! This life will not last forever!"[16]

White Bull's bold act of bravery was a bit showy, even for the proudest young warrior; however, his coup probably inspired his comrades. It likely also brought fear to the hearts of the soldiers who were unsuccessful in hitting White Bull. How, they must have thought, can we cope with an enemy that is willing to take such foolhardy chances? White Bull counted 6 other coups that day. He also killed 2 soldiers and captured 12 horses. The pony he rode was later killed in battle and White Bull suffered an ankle wound.

Back on the western side of Battle Ridge, where the Gray Horse Troop had made its downhill deployment, the soldiers and warriors awaited the next move. After it appeared that Company E was not going to press its charge further, the warriors responded with an intense counterattack.

The same age as Custer, Lame White Man led this charge. He was at the time 37 years old, a Southern Cheyenne adopted into a Northern Cheyenne community. He was accompanied by hundreds of Cheyenne and Sioux warriors, including 20 young men whom historian Gregory F. Michno has termed "the suicide boys." During a ceremonial dance held the night before, these teenagers made a suicide vow that they would fight to the death in their next battle. Included among this group were the Northern Cheyenne warriors Cut Belly, Closed Hand, Limber Bones, Roman Nose, Noisy Walking, and Little Whirlwind. Also with Lame White Man were the experienced warriors Contrary Belly, Yellow Nose, Comes In Sight, and others.

Lame White Man's war party rushed up the gullies and around the ridges. It encircled the Gray Horse Troop in a matter of minutes, getting as close as 40 feet to the vulnerable soldiers. Wolf Tooth and Big Foot led their Cheyenne party to the ridgeline area where Company E had previously been deployed. From that position, they had a clear line to fire down on the soldiers. Runs the Enemy and another party of 30 warriors charged down from the ridge and stampeded a number of the held horses. The famous grays of Company E galloped to the Little Bighorn River, where they stopped to quench their thirst. The warriors counted coup by capturing the horses and all the supplies they carried, including ammunition and blankets.

Many soldiers were killed as the warriors seized the initiative. Most of the survivors of the counterattack scurried on foot back up the gulch with warriors in pursuit. Some of the men ran for cover in Deep Ravine. Most of the 40-man company never made it back to the ridge; its commander, Algernon Smith, did survive to fight in the final battle, though.

A platoon of cavalrymen, perhaps from Yates's Company F, moved to the top of the gulch to cover the retreat of the Company E survivors. The "suicide boys" mounted a fierce attack against another platoon on what are today the cemetery grounds. The survivors of this attack, also likely from Company F, scampered to Last Stand Hill. The fighting was intense during the Lame White Man counterattack. Wolf Tooth recalled that there was hand-to-hand combat and that warriors used hatchets, spears, and clubs in addition to firearms. Rain in the Face reported that the soldiers fired their guns as rapidly as they could load them, while the warriors mostly shot arrows.

TURNING POINT

The casualties were not at all one-sided, as many warriors were also killed or wounded. Wooden Leg recalled that more warriors were taken out during the ravine counterattack "than fell at any other one section of the field."[17] Near the top of the ridge, Lame White Man himself was hit and later died of his wounds. (He was one of only 30 to 40 of the villagers who died from combat wounds.) The suicide boys Cut Belly, Closed Hand, Limber Bones, and Noisy Walking were also killed in action. It appears, however, that the real suicide boys were wearing blue coats. Both Antelope and Wooden Leg witnessed panicked soldiers who took their own lives.

The Gray Horse Troop's ill-fated charge marked an important turning point in the battle. Prior to this retreat, Custer's five companies had been on the offensive. Now they were forced to assume a defensive posture. Cavalry units were most effective as a mobile strike force on level ground. On the Battle Ridge, the capability of Custer's battalion was now reduced to reacting to further warrior charges. The terrain was uneven and the field of fire was poor. Few, if any, natural barriers could protect them, and their horses often became a disadvantage. More critically, they faced a force that had greater numbers, firepower, mobility, and elusiveness.

At around 5:40 P.M., the counterattack finished driving the Company E survivors back to the ridge. At about this same time, warriors led by White Bull and Crazy Horse started a ride from the east against part of Keogh's wing above Calhoun Hill. This was more like a reaction to a dare than it was an attack. White Bull, who previously rode through the skirmish line, challenged Crazy Horse to demonstrate his bravery. Crazy Horse immediately started racing his horse toward the soldiers. White Bull followed close behind. Their dash inspired many other warriors to join the run. Probably to the surprise of the U.S. troops, the chargers split the line between companies L and C and continued to the top of the ridge. What started as a feat of bravery turned into a major penetration of the U.S. forces and marked the beginning of the rapid decline of Custer's remaining defenses.

The penetration of the line rattled the troopers so badly that they were unable to respond effectively. Their instinct to flee won over their desire to fight. Those north of the break in the line began moving toward Last Stand Hill. Those south of the break started toward Calhoun Hill. Some headed to the west side of the ridge toward the river. It was at this point in the battle when numerous Native American eyewitnesses first mention soldiers fleeing the battlefield. The shock of the attack was so great that many of the once-confident troops thought that escape was the only way to save their own lives. The panic even drove a few beyond the point of self-preservation, to choose suicide over death at the hands of charging warriors.

At about the same time that Crazy Horse and White Bull's band broke through the soldiers' line from the west, another group of warriors assaulted the Calhoun Hill skirmish line of Company L from the south. The Hunkpapa warrior Gall rallied this war party, which vastly outnumbered the soldiers. According to Gall, the warriors easily overwhelmed the skirmish line and crested the hill. "We either killed or ran over these [cavalrymen] and went on down to where the last soldiers were."[18]

As the surviving soldiers left their position and headed northward, the warriors took over the hilltop. This left the Company C platoon on Finley Ridge in a hopeless position. Their left flank began to receive fire from two directions. One was from the warriors now atop Calhoun Hill. The other was from a group of warriors east and south of Calhoun Hill in a position now called Henryville. This position was named in the mid-1980s by archeologists after they discovered a large artifact collection there, which included

Like Sitting Bull, Hunkpapa warrior Gall did not accept the terms of the Fort Laramie Treaty of 1868, which called for all western Sioux to settle on the Great Sioux Reservation. After the Battle of the Little Bighorn, Gall fled to Canada with Sitting Bull.

numerous .44-caliber Henry cartridges. The number of cartridges indicated that about 20 warriors at this position were using .44-caliber Henry repeating rifles. These weapons were less powerful than the cavalry's Springfield rifles, especially at long range; however, they had the advantage of providing rapid fire. They could fire many shots in succession by the use of a lever, whereas the Springfield had to be reloaded by hand after each single shot. The rapid firepower of the Henry repeaters was intimidating, especially to inexperienced soldiers. Their use was probably a significant cause of the confusion and panic among the soldiers so widely reported by Native American eyewitnesses. The firing from Henryville certainly persuaded the men on Finley Ridge to quickly abandon their position. Survivors of the assaults on Calhoun Hill and Finley Ridge fled north to seek safety with Keogh's Company I. These troops were located several hundred yards above Calhoun Hill on the eastern slope of Battle Ridge.

Company I deployed to face the warriors pursuing the survivors from the south and west; however, they could not react quickly enough to prevent the disintegration of their own unit. Warriors led by Crazy Horse then swept in from the east, attacking all three of Captain Keogh's companies. This wing of the battalion was surrounded and cut down. Several Native American eyewitnesses, including the warriors Runs the Enemy and Little Hawk, likened the fighting in the Keogh sector to a buffalo chase. Julia Face, daughter of the Oglala leader Face and wife of the Brulé warrior Thunder Hawk, witnessed the final phases of battle from the Oglala cluster in the village. The warriors, she recalled, "acted like they were driving buffalo to a good place to be slaughtered."[19]

To cover the retreat of Company C, Calhoun's Company L shifted its southern skirmish line toward the west. Sioux and Northern Cheyenne warriors took advantage of this movement to launch a charge toward Calhoun Hill from the south. They rushed forward with an intense burst of rifle fire. The sudden shock of the attack caused Company C's skirmish line to quickly collapse. A few panicked soldiers tried to escape. This encouraged more warriors to join the charge. They raced in from several directions, both mounted and on foot.

The most intense fighting of the entire battle then followed. More Native American warriors died in the fight for Calhoun Hill than anywhere else on the battlefield. U.S. troops who tried to flee were run down. Those who attempted to bunch together became easy targets for warrior arrows. Lieutenant Calhoun was killed in one of these small, bunched groups. Some of the fleeing soldiers on horseback managed to ride the 600 yards north to Company I's position. Most of those on foot were run down and killed by warriors.

CAPTAIN MYLES WALTER KEOGH: IRISH SOLDIER OF FORTUNE

Myles Walter Keogh (1842–1876) was an Irish soldier of fortune whose three-company battalion was annihilated in the Battle Ridge sector of the Little Bighorn battlefield. Born in County Carlow, Ireland, to a staunchly Catholic family with 12 other children, he was one of the 7th Cavalry's more colorful characters. Following two years of college, he left Ireland to become a mercenary officer in the Papal Army. After unsuccessfully fighting the revolutionary Italian forces of Garibaldi, Pope Pius IX awarded him two medals of valor, which he was wearing when he died. Keogh immigrated to the United States in 1862 to join the U.S. Army and fight in the Civil War. He was given the temporary rank of major after serving with distinction in the Battle of Gettysburg. A dapper dresser, who always carried a swagger stick with a silver dog's head handle, he gained a reputation as a ladies' man but never married.

Less than a mile to the north, Custer must have witnessed in horror the annihilation of Keogh's unit. There was nothing he could do to help. Companies E and F were pinned down and too far out of range to provide supporting fire. They also did not have a chance to react. Within minutes, most of Keogh's command was wiped out.

The sights and sounds of chaos filled the battlefield. The air was filled with gun smoke, dust, yells of charging warriors, and screams of wounded men and horses. More soldiers tried to group together before either being killed or forced to flee. Captain Keogh and some of his men were killed on the eastern slope of the ridge. Keogh himself was shot off the back of his horse Comanche. His horse was later discovered to be the only remnant of Custer's battalion still alive on Last Stand Hill.

The fleeing soldiers moved north from Calhoun Hill to Last Stand Hill. Many were on foot. More dead horses were discovered in this area than in any other part of the battle-field. Only a handful of the men of Keogh's wing made it to the temporary shelter of Custer's wing. At this point, warriors hoisted three company guidons as coup-sticks. Dead soldiers in the wake of the fight were stripped of their weapons and other trophies. The wounded were put out of their misery. More than half of Custer's battalion was dead. The remaining two intact companies were encircled and outnumbered.

Captain Yates's Company E deployed to receive the Keogh wing survivors. The company set a skirmish line and opened fire on the pursuing warriors, momentarily halting their advance. The slightly more than 100 soldiers left in the battalion were positioned near Cemetery Ridge and Last Stand Hill. They were surrounded and outnumbered, perhaps by as many as 20 to 1. There was no sign from the Reno and Benteen battalions whom Custer had ordered to join his troops. Companies E and F moved to the top of Last Stand Hill. This proved to be a poor position as thousands of warriors pressed a final attack.

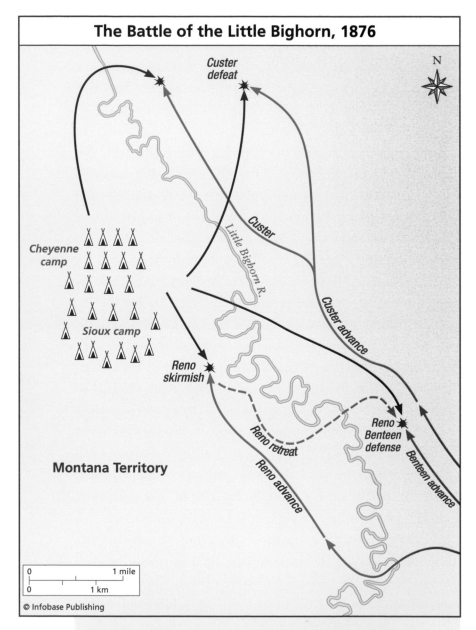

The Battle of the Little Bighorn, 1876

Custer
defeat

N

Cheyenne
camp

Custer

Little Bighorn R.

Custer advance

Sioux camp

Reno
skirmish

Reno retreat

Reno
Benteen
defense

Benteen advance

Montana Territory

Reno advance

0   1 mile
0   1 km

© Infobase Publishing

Possible Native American and U.S. Army troop movements
are depicted in this map of the Battle of the Little Bighorn.
(Historians differ on the specific Custer route.) The battle
resulted in the death of 268 U.S. Army cavalrymen and 30 to 40
Native American villagers in what has become one of the most
studied military conflicts in American history.

The hilltop was surrounded and the warriors were moving in closer. Some men killed horses to serve as defensive barriers they could hide behind. Most of the other horses were set free in the hope that warriors would follow in chase. This desperate plan did not work. Then, perhaps because they could now see Captain Weir's men down at Weir Point, about a dozen soldiers decided to make a run toward the river. Brave Wolf, a Northern Cheyenne war chief, stated that warriors "killed them all going down the hill, before any of them got to the creek. . . . It was hard fighting, very hard all the time. I have been in many hard fights, but I never saw such brave men."[20]

All that remained now of Custer's battalion were the 42 soldiers still fighting on Last Stand Hill. Perhaps they consisted of those too wounded or exhausted to escape and some able-bodied men too loyal to abandon their struggling comrades. Although the end result of the fight was by then obvious to the warriors, many recalled that it still required fierce action to bring it to an end. The Two Kettle warrior Runs the Enemy, who had been in battle all afternoon, also participated in this final fight. He recalled:

> The soldiers then gathered in a group . . . and then the soldiers and Indians were all mixed up. You could not tell one from the other. In this final charge I took part and when the last soldier was killed the smoke rolled up like a mountain above our heads, and soldiers were piled one on top of another, dead, and here and there an Indian among the soldiers.[21]

A LAST STAND?

One of the most controversial issues in modern scholarship of the Little Bighorn battle is whether or not Custer and his men made a "Last Stand" on Last Stand Hill. Based on his extensive study of battlefield artifacts, archeologist Richard A.

Fox Jr. concluded that the battle had "no famous last stand."[22] Fox took the stance that a last-stand scenario was a myth because the evidence indicated that Custer's tactical position disintegrated too quickly to be viewed as a defensive stand.

Certainly there was no superheroic last stand as has been portrayed in many movies, paintings, and literary works. Errol Flynn's role as Custer in the 1941 movie *They Died with Their Boots On* typifies this mythic portrayal. As hundreds of warriors encircle him and his men lie dying at his feet, Flynn's Custer stands erect next to the regimental guidon with his saber drawn, rapidly firing his pistol. Finally, he is hit with a fatal bullet, clutches his chest, and collapses. As befits only the rarest of legendary military heroes, Custer is thus the last of his men to make a stand.

Although there was no Hollywood-style last stand, the Sioux and Northern Cheyenne participants recall that Custer's two companies fought for more than an hour from positions on or near Cemetery Ridge. Most of the Native American eyewitnesses of the fight recalled that the soldiers did make a stand and defended their ground fiercely until the end. This testimony and other evidence suggests that the surviving soldiers made several "stands," and since they all died in battle, one of these stands had to be "last." Soldiers inflicted the vast majority of casualties on warriors in the northern portion of Custer's battlefield. The results of their shooting and the duration of their fighting indicates that they defended their position as long as was humanly possible. The battle on Last Stand Hill was over by about 6:10 P.M.

Custer's body was found on top of another dead soldier and horse. There were bullet holes in his chest and right temple. On the ground were 17 shells from his Remington sporting rifle. Close by were the bodies of his brothers Tom and Boston. Tom had been shot full of arrows. Also among the 42 bodies found on Last Stand Hill were company commanders Captain George Yates and Lieutenant Algernon Smith, and adjutant Lieutenant William Cooke, who had scribbled the message to Benteen delivered by Private John Martin. Cooke was distinguished by a long beard that he parted in the middle. The warrior Wooden Leg claimed that he scalped one side of Cooke's face and attached the hair to a shaft of an arrow. As was the custom, he gave this war trophy to his grandmother. She was reportedly spooked by the strange scalp, though, and soon discarded it.

Warriors and women who went to the battle site stripped Custer's troopers of their clothing and gear. Some of the bodies were badly butchered, especially by women who took revenge for lost husbands, brothers, or sons. However, most were not severely mutilated. The Cheyenne woman Antelope (Kate Bighead) later claimed that Custer had received other wounds. She related that two Southern Cheyenne women recognized him from his campaign in Indian Territory (Oklahoma) in the late 1860s. According to the tribe's oral tradition, Custer had an affair during that period with Monahsetah, the teenaged daughter of Chief Little Rock, and was believed to have fathered a child by her. Knowing of this alleged relationship, the two women prevented Sioux warriors from mutilating Custer's body. They explained in sign language that they considered him to be a relative. According to Antelope, after the warriors agreed to do no further harm to Custer's corpse:

> [The] women then pushed the point of a sewing awl into each of his ears, into his head. This was done to improve his hearing, as it seemed he had not heard what our chiefs in the South said when he smoked the pipe with them. They told him that if ever afterward he should break the peace promise and should fight the Cheyennes the Everywhere Spirit surely would cause him to be killed.[23]

Some skeptics think the Cheyennes made up this story. However, the officers who first examined Custer's body found bloodstains around his ears and an arrow forced up his penis. This may well have been the work of two Southern Cheyenne women who sought in bitterness to symbolize Custer's broken promises, both to a sister of their community and to their nation as a whole. In addition, Custer was responsible for the deaths of more than 100 Cheyenne villagers, mostly women and children, during the Washita Massacre.

Having defeated Custer, the warriors turned their attention to Captain Weir's unit, which they had observed on Weir Point. The company had made a poorly executed retreat back to Reno Hill, abandoning one of their wounded. The surrounded soldiers erected a makeshift fortification on the hilltop. They also set up a field hospital where Dr. Porter, the battalion's only surviving surgeon, treated the wounded and dying. Warriors continued to fire on the hill, killing five more men by nightfall. After the sun went down, most of the warriors returned to the village to celebrate their victory. On the morning of June 26, warriors converged to launch another attack on Reno Hill.

DAY TWO AND AFTERMATH

Although there were no overwhelming charges like those of the previous day, seven more soldiers died in the fighting. Captain Benteen led his Company H on a foot charge to the south, which succeeded in driving off a threatening group of warriors on the perimeter. Later, a group of volunteers proceeded down to a source of water in what became known as "Water Carriers' Ravine." Covered by the rifle fire of sharpshooters, the volunteers filled canteens for their thirsty comrades on the hill. Several of the water carriers and the riflemen who covered their trail later received the Congressional Medal of Honor for their deeds. The Sioux and their allies were unwilling to continue an assault against the well-defended Reno Hill. Word had spread that General Terry's column was approaching the area from the north. That afternoon, the soldiers on the hilltop observed the people of the village setting fire to the prairie grass and breaking camp. As Sergeant Charles Windolph of Company H described the scene:

> The heavy smoke seemed to lift for a few moments, and there in the valley below we caught glimpses of thousands of Indians on foot and horseback, with their pony herds and travois, dogs, and pack animals, and all the trappings of a great camp, slowly moving southward. It was like a Biblical Exodus; the Israelites moving out of Egypt; a mighty tribe on the march.[24]

The German-born Windolph was one of the Reno Hill sharpshooters who received the Congressional Medal of Honor. He also gained the distinction of being the U.S. Army's longest-living survivor of the Little Bighorn battle. He died in 1950 at age 98.

By the time that Terry's column arrived to rescue the men on Reno Hill on June 27, only three covered tepees remained standing on the scorched earth of Sitting Bull's former village. These were funeral sites for the bodies of fallen tribal members.

A shocked General Terry rode to Reno Hill to spread the first word of the fate of Custer's battalion. A burial party found Custer and his men on Last Stand Hill. The dead leader had commanded one of the most complete military disasters in American history. His colossal defeat immediately set off an endless stream of debate, controversy, and speculation that continues to fascinate a wide audience throughout the world. Custer sought and gained fame throughout his life and probably could have achieved much more if he had lived beyond the age of 37. Yet it was by failure that he achieved immortality.

For the Sioux and Cheyennes, the Battle of the Little Big-horn symbolized the peak of their power as warrior nations and of the plains culture that supported their freedom. Yet the glory days and the old ways were not destined to last much longer. It took another 15 years and several more battles before the Sioux and Cheyennes were forced to acknowledge the reality of their defeat as nations. The seeds of doom that led to the ultimate loss of their military and cultural war were firmly planted on the battlefield of their greatest victory.

The Road to Wounded Knee, 1876–1890

News of the Little Bighorn battle reached the public just before July 4, the date on which an elaborate celebration was to be held in Philadelphia to mark the United States' centennial year. Shocked and outraged citizens, politicians, and newspaper reporters demanded an explanation from the U.S. Army, as well as swift retribution against the Native Americans who fought in the battle. The U.S. Army responded by launching an investigation of the military "blunder." It also dispatched a significant portion of its manpower to hunt down the victorious warriors. The investigation looked for someone to blame for the defeat, but found no one guilty of a military offense. The U.S. Army generally skirted the issue of the tactical failure of the 7th Cavalry.

General Philip H. Sheridan ordered all tribal members on the reservations to surrender their horses and weapons. The U.S. Army's loss at Little Bighorn also provided a good excuse for taking the sacred Paha Sapa away from the tribes. A government commission pressured tribal leaders into selling the Black Hills by threatening the withdrawal of rations of food, clothing, and supplies. The forced "agreement" reached in October 1877 not only separated the Black Hills from the Great Sioux Reservation, it also forced the tribes to give up their hunting grounds in the unceded territory. In 1980, the U.S. Supreme Court ruled that the Black Hills agreement was illegal and that the Sioux tribes were entitled to more than $100 million in damages. For more than a quarter century, the tribes have refused to accept this monetary settlement, demanding instead that their land be returned.

On September 9, 1876, a cavalry unit attached to General Crook's column attacked the Minneconjou village led by American Horse within the Great Sioux Reservation. The warrior American Horse had participated in the Little Bighorn battle. His village was located near Slim Buttes, a landmark rock formation near present-day Reva, South Dakota. After receiving word of the attack while at a camp 10 miles to the south, Crazy Horse gathered a party of up to 800 warriors and quickly rode to the village.

When the warriors arrived, they discovered the remainder of General Crook's column at the scene. After an extensive firefight, the soldiers drove off the warriors, burned the village, and seized the ponies and food supply. The soldiers also recovered a number of artifacts from the Little Bighorn battle, including a 7th Cavalry guidon and bloody gloves belonging to Captain Keogh. American Horse and at least nine other Sioux died in the Battle of Slim Buttes. The soldiers lost two cavalrymen and a civilian scout.

In October 1876, an expedition commanded by Colonel Nelson Miles (known to the Sioux as "Bear Coat") chased down almost 2,000 Minneconjou and Sans Arc tribal members in Montana and convinced them to surrender. The Hunkpapas who followed Sitting Bill, Gall, and the Sans Arcs led by Spotted Eagle then fled north to Canada.

On November 25, 1876, Colonel Ranald S. Mackenzie led a huge U.S. Army column in a dawn attack against the

Northern Cheyenne village led by Dull Knife and Little Wolf in Wyoming. This village, consisting of 200 lodges, was located along Bates Creek near the northern fork of the Powder River. The invading force of 1,100 men included troops from four cavalry regiments and an attachment of Pawnee warriors. The Cheyennes put up a fierce resistance, but were eventually forced to abandon the village and all their possessions and flee into the frozen countryside. Mackenzie's force burned the camp and captured several hundred ponies. At least 30 Cheyenne tribal members were killed in battle. Lacking blankets, 12 babies also froze to death that night. The U.S. Army lost five enlisted men and one officer.

SURRENDER OF "THE ROAMERS"

The Dull Knife Fight (also known as the Battle of Bates Creek) convinced most of the Cheyennes to surrender. Those who continued to maintain the will to fight found refuge in Crazy Horse's camp. In January 1877, the Sioux and Cheyennes who followed Crazy Horse tried to lure Colonel Miles into a trap.

The commander and his troops were looking for the Native Americans in the Tongue River Valley of Wyoming. The warriors sprung the ambush too soon, and so the soldiers were able to capture a number of Cheyenne women and children. At dawn on January 8, Crazy Horse led 500 warriors against Miles's position in an effort to free the hostages. The U.S. Army fought them off with heavy artillery fire and well-placed sharpshooters. This Battle of Wolf Mountain ended around noon when a blizzard made it impossible to see the field. The demoralized warriors withdrew from the fight, which proved to be the last for Crazy Horse.

By April, nearly all of the roamers had decided that the comparative safety and free rations of the reservation was a better option than dodging soldiers' bullets. In May, Crazy Horse led his nearly 1,500 Oglala followers to surrender at the Red Cloud Agency on the Great Sioux Reservation. Also

In May 1877, Crazy Horse, along with his band of 1,500 Oglala followers, surrendered to the U.S. Army at Camp Robinson on the Great Sioux Reservation. Despite his desire for peace, Crazy Horse was killed exactly four months later by an army private when he resisted arrest at Camp Robinson.

in April, Colonel Miles and his soldiers chased after Lame Deer's band of Minneconjous in Montana. Surprisingly, some of the scouts who assisted the U.S. Army in this hunt were Sioux and Cheyenne tribal leaders who had been at Little Bighorn. These included Hump, a fellow Minneconjou, the Oglala Short Bull, and the Cheyennes Brave Wolf and Ice (also known as White Bull). Miles's unit attacked Lame Deer's camp at Little Muddy Creek, a tributary of the Rosebud Creek. Lame Deer and 14 of his people were killed in the battle. The remainder of his camp escaped.

The Cheyenne leader Ice distinguished himself at this Battle of Little Muddy Creek, both by saving Colonel Miles's life and by taking the scalps of Lame Deer and his cousin. His deeds serve as an example of the U.S. Army's successful efforts in pressuring some Native Americans to consider their former allies as enemies. Ice, the older brother of Antelope (Kate Bighead), was a leading spiritual leader in the Little Bighorn village and did not take part in the fighting. However, his only son, 18-year-old Noisy Walking, was one of the Cheyenne "suicide boys" killed during the attack.

By September 1877, the last surviving holdouts of Lame Deer's camp straggled into the reservation agencies. Sitting Bull's followers in Canada were the only Sioux who continued to enjoy the traditional freedom of the roamers. In the meantime, though, Crazy Horse was causing tension on the reservation. He was mad that his people had not been given their own reservation in Montana as had been promised. He was also upset that some warriors agreed to serve as scouts for the U.S. Army. Fearing Crazy Horse would start a rebellion, General Crook ordered that he be arrested.

Crazy Horse and his family fled the Red Cloud Agency, but other Oglalas escorted them back on September 6, 1877. When Crazy Horse realized that the building he was being led to at Camp Robinson in Nebraska was the military stockade, or jail, a scuffle broke out. Crazy Horse pulled a knife, and his childhood friend Little Big Man tried to restrain him. A soldier ran forward and stabbed Crazy Horse twice in the back with a bayonet, a long knife attached to the barrel of a rifle.

Crazy Horse died from his wounds later that day. That night, his father, Worm, retrieved the corpse and carried it in a wagon to a bluff near Beaver Creek in northwestern Nebraska. In a crevice in the rocks, the grieving parents hid the body of one of the most outstanding Native American warriors in history. This burial place remains unknown, and therefore undisturbed, to this day.

Angered by the death of their leader, some of Crazy Horse's followers fled the reservation and joined Sitting Bull's holdouts in Canada. But life proved grim for the roamers north of the international border. The Royal Canadian

Mounted Police watched their every move, and the U.S. Army scouted the border for an opportunity to capture them. Food and supplies became scarce, especially during the long, brutal winters. After five years in exile, Sitting Bull was finally convinced in the summer of 1881 that the effort to retain the old way of life was futile.

On July 19, 1881, Sitting Bull and his remaining followers surrendered at Fort Buford on the Missouri River in present-day North Dakota. In a council the next day at post headquarters, the Hunkpapa leader formally addressed Major David H. Brotherton, the post commander: "I surrender this rifle to you through my young son, whom I now desire to teach in this manner that he has become a friend of the Americans. . . . I wish it to be remembered that I was the last man of my tribe to surrender my rifle."[25]

Sitting Bull was held prisoner for two years at Fort Randall in what is today South Dakota. His Hunkpapa followers were assigned to the reservation's Standing Rock Agency in present-day North Dakota. Having been dispossessed of their sacred Black Hills, their western hunting grounds, and most of their fertile lands east of the Missouri River, the tribal members of the recently mighty Sioux warrior nation were by this time settled on some of the least-valuable land on the Great Plains. Life on the reservation soon proved miserable for them. Poorly fed and clothed, they witnessed the disappearance of many vestiges of their traditional way of life. The values and customs of their warrior culture lost meaning once wealth and prestige could no longer be attained through raiding and combat. The economic and material basis of this culture collapsed once buffalo could no longer be hunted. It was a profound psychological blow.

Moreover, the policies implemented by the Office of Indian Affairs did not help ease the adjustment. The goal of the U.S. government's reservation policy was to "civilize" tribal members. This was to be accomplished by converting them to Christianity, educating them in Euro-American culture and values, and training them to become farmers or ranchers on their own land. To facilitate this latter program, tribal members were eventually allotted parcels of up to 320 acres of land for their individual use and ownership.

Local agents followed the stated federal policy of preparing tribal members for U.S. citizenship by undermining the power and influence of their recognized tribal leaders and councils. They outlawed native religious and medical practices, including the Sun Dance and other dances and feasts, and the use of traditional medicine men and healing ceremonies. The agents also made tribal members economically dependent on government rations, which in turn killed the incentive for finding other opportunities.

In addition, the land area of the Great Sioux Reservation was drastically reduced over time. In 1889, the government divided the one large reservation into five smaller and separate reservations: Cheyenne River, Lower Brulé, Pine Ridge, Rosebud, and Standing Rock. After land parcels on these reservations were allotted to individual tribal members, the lands remaining (so-called surplus lands) were opened to Euro-American homesteaders. Although today much smaller in size, these five Sioux reservations continue to exist in North and South Dakota.

After Sitting Bull was released from confinement and spent some time at his new home on Standing Rock, he left the reservation to try to take advantage of his fame in the wider world. For a brief period beginning in 1883, he became a show-business celebrity after discovering that there was a demand for his appearance at public events. He also learned that he could sell his autograph for up to $2 per signing. In 1884, Sitting Bull was the headliner in a touring show described as depicting "wild life of the plains." The stage group also included Flying By and other Sioux warriors who had fought at the Little Bighorn. The show opened in New York City and played to packed houses for two weeks.

The next year, Sitting Bull became a feature of "Buffalo Bill's Wild West." This was a popular traveling circus organized by William F. Cody. The tour stopped at more than a dozen cities in the United States and Canada. The Hunkpapa leader was not sensationalized as the "slayer of Custer" nor in mock battles of Little Bighorn, as some accounts have maintained. Rather, Cody presented him merely as a famous chief and had him ride in parades and greet visitors in a tepee. Sitting Bull enjoyed the experience and used all of his earnings to sponsor feasts for his friends. However, his brief show-business career ended after only one season with Buffalo Bill when James McLaughlin, the government agent at Standing Rock, refused to allow him to go out on tour again.

Having witnessed some of the seamy side of the Euro-American world as a result of his show tours, Sitting Bull shared his thoughts with the missionary Mary Collins: "I want you to teach my people to read and write but they must not become white people in their ways; it is too bad a life, I could not let them do it. I would rather die an Indian than live a white man."[26]

THE GHOST DANCE MOVEMENT

Afflicted with despair, misery, and depression, the Sioux people on the reservations found themselves eagerly receptive when news reached them of the appearance of a Native American messiah in Nevada. Wovoka, a Paiute shaman also known as Jack Wilson, began preaching new religious concepts in 1889. He claimed that during a total eclipse of the sun on the first day of that year, he had a significant death experience. He was transported to heaven, where he visited with and received instructions from God, after which he was returned to Earth to spread the word of a glorious new life for native people.

In 1890, Chief Kicking Bear brought the Ghost Dance to the Sioux, who eagerly embraced the religion after years of despair. The religious movement professed that only Native Americans would inhabit a new world where game was plentiful and people would live free of want, sickness, and discomfort.

The teachings and visions that Wovoka shared were a mixture of both Christian and Native American beliefs. His concepts, which included the coming of a Native American promised land in the near future, became known as the Ghost Dance religion. According to Wovoka's vision, only Native Americans, including ancestors brought back to life, would inhabit the new world. Buffalo and all other game would again be plentiful and all people would dwell happily and forever free of want, sickness, and discomfort. To bring about this millennium, Wovoka advised that the people must believe in him and follow the rituals God had showed him, including a special dance that would bring back the "ghosts" of their ancestors. They must also keep the tenets of the faith. These included an emphasis on pacifism and the rejection of Euro-American ways, especially the consumption of alcohol. "You must not fight," Wovoka advised. "Do no harm to anyone. Do right always."[27]

In the autumn of 1889, leaders of the Sioux tribes sent a delegation of 11 men to the Paiute reservation on the Walker River in western Nevada to meet with Wovoka and confirm reports heard about his prophecy. Of these men, Kicking Bear and Short Bull became the leading disciples of the Ghost Dance among the Sioux.

Kicking Bear, a nephew of Sitting Bull, was an Oglala medicine man. He was married to Woodpecker Woman, a niece of the Minneconjou chief known as Big Foot. Kicking Bear lived with his wife's people on the Cheyenne River Reservation. As a warrior he had often ridden with the war parties of Crazy Horse, including at the Little Bighorn battle. He distinguished himself in that fight by killing many soldiers during Major Reno's retreat to the river.

Short Bull was a Brulé who lived on the Rosebud Reservation. He was also Kicking Bear's brother-in-law. Although he may have also fought at Little Bighorn, he should not be confused with the Oglala warrior of the same name who was among the leading warriors at both the Rosebud and Little Bighorn battles.

The Sioux delegates heard Wovoka's teachings and learned the dance that would hasten the new future. But Kicking Bear and Short Bull interpreted the prophet's message through the lens of their own warrior culture. They proclaimed that as punishment for the abuse of Native Americans, the vengeful messiah was going to violently destroy all the Euro-Americans in the spring of 1891. Many Sioux understood this to mean that the use of force would help bring about this time of deliverance.

The Sioux apostles of Wovoka also added a unique concept to their practice of the Ghost Dance. They taught that dancers were to wear specially designed garments known as Ghost Shirts. These sacklike shirts, painted with ancient Sioux symbols, were believed to have the miraculous quality of protecting their wearers by turning away bullets. This idea of a need for protection in future warfare was yet another way in which Wovoka's doctrine of peace became a doctrine of aggression in the minds of the Sioux followers of the Ghost Dance.

During the spring and summer of 1890, Kicking Bear and Short Bull spread the message of the new faith among their people. They had little success at first, but gained many converts by late July after a severe drought and a further reduction of government rations brought the Sioux close to starvation. Thereafter, a significant minority of tribal members on the Rosebud, Pine Ridge, and Cheyenne River reservations abandoned their homesteads to gather in camps near the creeks to participate in the rituals of the Ghost Dance.

Federal officials and white residents on or near the reservations became alarmed that this religious fervor would lead to an outbreak of violence. President Benjamin Harrison ordered an investigation of the situation in October 1890. In mid-November, Nelson Miles, now promoted to brigadier general and commander of the U.S. Army's Division of the Missouri, ordered five cavalry and eight infantry companies to proceed to the Rosebud and Pine Ridge reservations.

At Standing Rock, James McLaughlin, the government agent in charge, implicated Sitting Bull in the Ghost Dance activities and sought his arrest. Sitting Bull had not danced with or directed the Ghost Dancers, but he was tolerant and supportive of those who became converts. Agent McLaughlin had long been at odds with the Hunkpapa spiritual leader, and misinterpreted Sitting Bull's tolerance of the dancers as full support. Seeing an opportunity to rid himself of his longtime nemesis, he identified Sitting Bull to Washington officials as a leading apostle of the dance. He then requested permission to arrest him and have him transported to a military prison.

Prior to December 11, 1890, Sitting Bull received an invitation to join Kicking Bear and Short Bull and the most zealous Ghost Dancers at a camp in the *Makoce Sica* (Badlands of South Dakota) known as the Stronghold. This camp was on elevated tableland naturally protected by steep cliffs and supported by ample water and green grass for grazing animals. On the night of December 11, Sitting Bull dictated a letter to McLaughlin, advising him of his decision to accept the invitation to Makoce Sica. McLaughlin ordered that Sitting Bull be arrested before he could depart for the Stronghold.

At dawn on December 15, 1890, a group of 44 Indian policemen and volunteers arrived at Sitting Bull's cabin and seized him. Lieutenant Bull Head, another Hunkpapa Agency veteran of the Little Bighorn battle, commanded the agency police who were known as the *Ceska Maza*. Bull Head had no love for Sitting Bull or for Catch the Bear, one of the chief's most devoted followers. When the policemen Bull Head, Red Tomahawk, and Shave Head escorted Sitting Bull out of his cabin, they found the other policemen surrounded by Sitting Bull's family and friends. Catch the Bear told the police that the people were not going to allow Sitting Bull's arrest. Sitting Bull's 14-year-old-son Crow Foot urged his father to resist.

When Sitting Bull abruptly stopped walking, his police escorts started pushing and pulling him. Suddenly, Catch the Bear shouldered a rifle and shot Bull Head, the police commander. Bull Head fell to the ground and shot Sitting Bull in the chest as he went down. Red Tomahawk then fired a bullet into the back of Sitting Bull's head. The renowned Hunkpapa medicine man, who was then about 59 years of age, died instantly.

Others soon joined the shootout, and within a few minutes, five policemen and six of Sitting Bull's family members and friends, including Catch the Bear, also received fatal wounds. When the firing stopped, policemen found Crow Foot hiding under a pile of blankets in his father's cabin. They asked the mortally wounded police chief Bull Head what they should do with the boy. He replied bitterly, "Do what you like with him, he is one of them that has caused this trouble."[28] The officers then executed their young fellow tribesman on the spot.

The remaining policemen tossed Sitting Bull's corpse into a wagon and piled the dead policemen on top of him. They then completed their mission of bringing the leader back to the Standing Rock agency. The dead policemen were buried with full military honors in the post cemetery at Fort Yates. Sitting Bull was buried in a nearby pauper's grave without ceremony, prayers, or family in attendance. This was a sad and ironic ending for the charismatic man who was one of the most famous Native American spiritual leaders in history.

A few years later, Sitting Bull's cabin and the gray circus horse given to him by Buffalo Bill were transported to Chicago and displayed at the 1903 World's Fair. But less is known about what actually happened to his remains. The original burial site was vandalized several times. Descendants of Sitting Bull claimed that in 1953 they moved his remains from Fort Yates to a memorialized site near present-day Mobridge, South Dakota. Some historians, however, maintain that at least some of his remains are still at the original gravesite in North Dakota. Yet, there is also the possibility that the Fort Yates grave was robbed prior to 1953 and that the real remains are buried elsewhere or no longer exist.

WOUNDED KNEE

Following the shootout at Sitting Bull's cabin, 400 of the Hunkpapa Ghost Dancers fled south from the reservation at Standing Rock to the Cheyenne River Reservation of the Minneconjou in South Dakota. Although most were convinced to surrender, 38 of this group accepted an invitation to join Chief Big Foot's camp on the Cheyenne River near Deep Creek.

Big Foot was a half brother of Sitting Bull. At the Battle of the Little Bighorn, he was one of the two main Minneconjou chiefs. He and his followers had participated in the Ghost Dance at the Cherry Creek camp of the Minneconjou leader Hump, and many of these people remained true believers. But Big Foot became disillusioned after Hump disavowed the new religion early in December. Hump had been one of the prominent warriors at Little Bighorn and was wounded in the fight for Calhoun Hill. After 1877, he became the chief of police at the Cheyenne River Reservation.

Although Big Foot shunned the Ghost Dance, the knowledge of his participation prompted General Miles to put him under watch and eventually to order his arrest. Lieutenant Colonel Edwin V. Sumner, the commander of U.S. Army troops at Cheyenne River, delayed action in the hope that the chief's reputation as a peacemaker could help prevent a hostile confrontation. After the Hunkpapa refugees and some of the dancers from Hump's camp joined Big Foot's camp, his village became alarmed by the large number of U.S. Army soldiers gathering in the area. Some of the men tried to persuade the chief to accept an invitation from Red Cloud and other Oglala leaders to come to the Pine Ridge Reservation in southwestern South Dakota. Red Cloud, who had not supported the Ghost Dance movement, hoped that Big Foot could restore good relations between bickering factions of the Oglala people. The chiefs offered 100 ponies to Big Foot for his diplomatic services.

Big Foot thought that his people should first go to Fort Bennett on the Missouri River to collect their rations and annuity goods. Tribal members, however, recollect that the chief was advised by the trader John "Red Beard" Dunn to head immediately for Pine Ridge because the U.S. Army

In December 1890, Red Cloud and other Oglala leaders invited Big Foot and his people to settle with them at Pine Ridge Reservation in southwestern South Dakota. Pictured here is an encampment of Brulés and Oglalas on the banks of White Clay Creek, which flows through the reservation.

was sending a thousand soldiers to his village. Thus, in the late afternoon of December 23, 1890, members of Big Foot's camp began a 100-mile trek to the southwest over rugged and frozen terrain toward Pine Ridge Reservation. The camp was composed of 350 tribal members, including 120 men and 230 women and children.

Big Foot was suffering from either a severe cold or influenza that turned into pneumonia during the journey. He was too sick to ride a horse and had to be transported in his wagon. He sent messengers ahead to inform the people at Pine Ridge that he was coming in peace but was ill. On the fourth day of the trek, the messengers returned to advise that Short Bull and Kicking Bear and the main body of militant Oglala and Brulé Ghost Dancers had voluntarily withdrawn from the Stronghold. These dancers were heading to the Pine Ridge Agency to surrender and they wanted Big Foot to time his travel so that all would arrive at the agency at the same time.

The messengers also reported that soldiers camped ahead on Big Foot's route near Wounded Knee Creek were searching for him. The headmen advised the chief to swing around them to the south. Big Foot, however, stated that he was too sick to make a longer journey. He insisted that they would continue in the same direction and take their chances.

General Nelson Miles misinterpreted the movement of Big Foot's camp. He thought it was headed to the Stronghold, where its presence might reignite the militants who had withdrawn from this dance site. From his field headquarters at Fort Meade, near present-day Rapid City, South Dakota, Miles ordered units of both the 6th and 9th Cavalry regiments to halt Big Foot's journey. These mounted soldiers were unsuccessful, because they scouted the wrong trails based on the assumption that Big Foot's destination was the Stronghold.

Meanwhile, Brigadier General John R. Brooke, a field commander headquartered at the Pine Ridge Agency, learned of Big Foot's message to the Oglalas that his people were heading to Brooke's location. Brooke immediately ordered Major Samuel M. Whitside of the 7th Cavalry regiment, Custer's old unit, to lead four troops (the new U.S. Army term for what were formerly called companies) of the regiment to search for Big Foot: "Find his trail and follow, or find his hiding place and capture him. If he fights, destroy him."[29]

Accompanied by a platoon from the 1st Artillery regiment and their cannon, Whitside's troops proceeded to the trading post near Wounded Knee Creek (a stream known to the Sioux as *Cankpe Opi Wakpala*). These were the encamped soldiers whom messengers had warned Big Foot about. Through U.S. Army scout interpreters, Big Foot conveyed the message that he would bring his people to Whitside's camp. However, Whitside, a seasoned veteran of the Apache wars, was not willing to leave anything to chance. He decided that the safest course was to have his full detachment of approximately 200 men ride out to meet Big Foot's band and escort his people to Wounded Knee.

On the afternoon of December 28, 1890, the soldiers confronted the traveling camp. Directed to Big Foot's wagon, Major Whitside peered down on the seriously ill leader wrapped in blankets. After Big Foot agreed to have his people escorted to Whitside's camp, the major arranged to have the chief transferred to the care of an army ambulance.

Whitside also wanted to confiscate the band's horses and guns; however, John Shangreau, his mixed-blood Oglala interpreter and chief of scouts, advised that any attempt to do so would lead to a fight. Better to wait, counseled Shangreau, until they got the band safely back to the U.S. Army camp.

Whitside escorted Big Foot's people to Wounded Knee and requested that additional troops be sent to help disarm the band. Upon receiving this request, General Brooke ordered Colonel James W. Forsyth, the commander of the 7th Cavalry, to march to Wounded Knee with an additional four troops (companies) of his unit and another artillery platoon. Forsyth's orders were to disarm "the prisoners" and march them to the railroad station at Gordon, Nebraska, from where they were to be shipped to a military prison in Omaha.

Forsyth had commanded the 7th Cavalry since 1886. He'd had a brilliant combat record during the Civil War, but had no command experience in any engagement with Native Americans. His men arrived at Wounded Knee at about 8:30 P.M. on the evening of December 28. Forsyth assumed command from Major Whitside, whose men already surrounded

On the evening of December 28, 1890, Colonel James W. Forsyth positioned four Hotchkiss guns on a hill overlooking Big Foot's camp at Wounded Knee, South Dakota. Pictured here are members of Battery E of the 1st Artillery, who, along with Forsyth's unit, would use these Hotchkiss guns during the massacre at Wounded Knee the following day.

Big Foot's people in the camp. The major had positioned two Hotchkiss guns on a hill overlooking the camp, with their barrels aimed at Big Foot's tepees. These were revolving-barrel machine guns capable of firing 43 rounds per minute with good accuracy from up to a mile away. After Colonel Forsyth arrived, he reinforced this hilltop battery with two more Hotchkiss guns.

The combined units of the 7th Cavalry at Wounded Knee included five officers who had fought at the Little Bighorn. The most notable of these men was Charles A. Varnum. Now a captain, Varnum had served as Custer's chief of scouts.

The U.S. Army commanders decided to delay the disarming of tribal members until the next morning. During the night, the officers consumed a keg of whiskey that Forsyth's men had brought to the camp to celebrate the capture of Big Foot.

After breakfast the next morning, all of the men of Big Foot's band were called to meet for a council in front of their leader's tepee. The soldiers of the regiment surrounded them in a square formation. Using interpreters, the cavalry officers first ordered the tribal members to surrender their weapons voluntarily. Then the officers began searching the tepees and the tribal members themselves. Big Foot's people became more upset and unruly as the search continued. Yellow Bird, a shaman who was a leader of the Minneconjou Ghost

CAPTAIN CHARLES A. VARNUM: LAST SURVIVING U.S. ARMY OFFICER OF LITTLE BIGHORN

Charles Albert Varnum (1849–1936) was one of the few officers of the 7th Cavalry who fought at both Little Bighorn and Wounded Knee. He was born into a prominent military family in Troy, New York, and graduated from the U.S. Military Academy in 1872. As a second lieutenant, he served as chief of scouts at Little Bighorn and advised Custer of the scout's observation of a large native village from Crow's Nest. Because he was attached to Major Reno's command, he survived the battle. As a captain at Wounded Knee, his pipe was shot out of his mouth during the massacre. He received the Congressional Medal of Honor for his heroic actions the following day protecting the troop withdrawal from White Clay Creek. Varnum retired as a colonel in 1919. When he died in San Francisco in 1936, at the age of 86, he was the last surviving officer of the Battle of the Little Bighorn.

Dancers, reportedly agitated the tribal members. He began dancing and praying, assuring the people that their Ghost Dance shirts would protect them.

The tension combined with the language barrier to ignite the situation. Big Foot's people were well aware that they were being confronted by the men of the 7th Cavalry, the unit that some of them had helped to defeat so soundly 14 years earlier. Many tribal members feared that the soldiers sought revenge. The soldiers were also nervous because most of them were inexperienced young men who had never faced any military combat. About 20 percent of the 419 enlisted men were recent recruits, and 38 of these recruits had enlisted only two weeks earlier.

Suddenly, a weapon was discharged in the air. Either Blue Mountain or Black Coyote may have fired it, perhaps accidentally. The former was Sitting Bull's deaf and mute stepson, who may not have understood what was taking place. As a young boy in 1876, Blue Mountain resided with his mother and other family members in Sitting Bull's lodge in the Little Bighorn village when it was attacked by Major Reno's troops. The latter, Black Coyote, was a Minneconjou who was described by fellow tribesman Turning Hawk as "a crazy man, a young man of very bad influence and in fact a nobody."[30] Black Coyote indeed demanded money before he would surrender his Winchester rifle, and the weapon may have gone off as two soldiers struggled to take it away from him.

At the same instant as the gun fired, the shaman Yellow Bird tossed a handful of dirt into the air. About a half-dozen young Sioux men who had not yet been searched then withdrew rifles hidden in their blankets and fired a volley into the soldiers of Troop K. Instinctively, the cavalrymen of Troops K and B returned fire toward the tribal men bunched together in front of Big Foot's tepee, most of whom were unarmed.

The council square exploded with the roar of gunfire and filled with clouds of smoke and dust and cries of pain and emotion. Some of the Sioux men fought hand to hand before deciding that escape from the square offered the only chance for survival. The shots that missed intended targets pierced the tepees of Big Foot's camp. Panic-stricken women and children scrambled to nearby roads in the wake of the camp's stampeding ponies. While some attempted to break away in wagons or on horseback, most sought shelter in nearby ravines or on the low banks of Wounded Knee Creek.

Colonel Forsyth charged up the hill to the battery of Hotchkiss artillery. Within moments the machine guns began raking the lodges of the Minneconjou camp, the fleeing tribal members, and the ravines and embankments where they sought shelter. The cavalry units also formed lines to spray fire at the same targets. Captain Edward S. Godfrey, who commanded Benteen's Company K at the Battle of the Little Bighorn, ordered the lines of his Troops C and D to commence firing. "They fired rapidly," he later recalled, "but it seemed to me only a few seconds till there was not a living thing before us."[31]

When the shooting stopped, Big Foot and most of his people were either dead or seriously wounded. Early in the exchange of gunfire, the chief was shot in the head as he lifted himself up from his sickbed. Yellow Bird, the shaman who had so much faith in the Ghost Dance, fought fiercely before he was also fatally wounded. Finding shelter in a military tent assigned to the scouts, he shot down several cavalrymen through a hole in the canvas. Once soldiers discovered the source of the fire, they sprayed the tent with rifle fire and Hotchkiss shells and set it on fire.

A regimental unit was assigned to gather up the dead and wounded soldiers, as well as the wounded Sioux, and transport them to the Pine Ridge Agency. Because the available barracks at the agency were soon filled with soldiers, the wounded tribal members had to remain in open wagons in the bitter cold until shelter was arranged at a nearby Episcopal mission. Due to a fast-approaching blizzard, the

Although the exact number of those who died at Wounded Knee is not known, some historians believe that as many as 300 of the approximately 350 members of Big Foot's band died during the massacre. Pictured here is Big Foot, whose frozen body was left in the snow for days.

7th Cavalry decided to leave the dead tribal members where they had fallen at Wounded Knee. When a burial party returned after the storm, they found the corpses, including that of Chief Big Foot, frozen into grotesque, contorted shapes. They piled the bodies on wagons and dumped them into a common grave.

The total number of Lakotas who died as a result of the Wounded Knee massacre is not known for certain. Some historians have speculated that as many as 300 of the approximately 350 members of Big Foot's band died from wounds or exposure or both. The U.S. Army's official body count from the battlefield totaled 146 tribal members, including 44 women and 18 children; 51 wounded were treated at the makeshift hospital at Pine Ridge, at least 7 of whom died later.

But it is likely that some of the dead were removed from the battlefield by relatives in advance of the burial party. It is also likely that many who escaped the field died elsewhere, especially if they had to endure both severe wounds and frigid weather without sufficient care or shelter.

An unknown number of the Minneconjou and Hunkpapa people at Wounded Knee on that fateful day in December 1890 had also been present at the Battle of the Little Bighorn. One individual who survived both conflicts was Iron Hail, a Minneconjou warrior who later became known as Dewey Beard (see his short biography on page 126). He was wounded in the arm and groin at Wounded Knee but continued to live until 1955, five years longer than the next-oldest survivor of the Little Bighorn battle.

The number of 7th Cavalry soldiers killed at Wounded Knee totaled 25. The dead included one officer, Captain George D. Wallace. A South Carolinian and West Point graduate, Wallace had been second in command of Company G during Reno's valley fight at Little Bighorn. A total of 37 soldiers and 2 civilians were wounded. The civilians were Philip Wells, a mixed-blood Sioux interpreter, and Father Francis Craft, a Catholic priest.

Although the 7th Cavalry suffered far fewer deaths and injuries in comparison to the Lakotas, its casualty rate of 1 out of every 8 men would have been considered high for an ordinary battle. It is likely that some of its casualties were the result of the crossfire of fellow soldiers in close quarters. However, the U.S. Army's casualty rate also reflected the intensity of the resistance offered by the outnumbered and overpowered Lakota fighters.

The public reaction to the events at Wounded Knee was mixed. The general notion that perhaps the majority of people carried away from newspaper reports was that the 7th Cavalry set up the battle to gain revenge for Custer's defeat at Little Bighorn. Many newspaper reports were critical of the U.S. Army's actions, describing the fight as an attack "on innocent victims" and a "slaughter without provocation."[32] General Nelson Miles, who later became the supreme commander of the U.S. Army, shared this view. He held Colonel John Forsyth responsible both for the massacre of women and children and for the deployment of his troops in a manner that resulted in crossfire casualties.

General Miles removed Forsyth from his command of the 7th Cavalry and appointed a court of inquiry to investigate his actions at Wounded Knee. The court, however, found Forsyth innocent of all charges. In 1894, Forsyth was promoted to brigadier general and he retired from the U.S. Army with the rank of major general.

Twenty soldiers and two artillery units were awarded the Congressional Medal of Honor for bravery in battle at

IRON HAIL (WASEE MAZA): LAST SURVIVOR OF LITTLE BIGHORN

Iron Hail (1857–1955), also known as Beard and Dewey Beard, was the last surviving warrior of the Little Bighorn battle. As a 17-year-old Minneconjou youth, he participated in a thwarted attack against Custer's unit on Last Stand Hill, armed with only a bow and arrows. As part of Big Foot's camp at Wounded Knee, he suffered wounds in his arm, chest, and leg. His parents, three siblings, and his wife were killed, and his infant son died a few months later of a battle-related illness. He eventually remarried, settled on Pine Ridge, and became a rancher. He adopted the name Dewey after meeting Admiral George Dewey, the naval hero of the Spanish-American War. During World War II, Beard's land allotment was condemned for use as an aerial gunnery range. As a result, he was landless when he died in 1955, thrice a victim of the U.S. Army.

Wounded Knee. This represents the most medals awarded for any single military engagement in U.S. history, including such major battles as the Normandy invasion of World War II. One of the officers so honored was Charles A. Varnum, who had been Custer's chief of scouts. When he died in 1936, Varnum was the last surviving U.S. Army officer of the Little Bighorn battle.

For many years, Native American activists have sought to have Congress recall the Wounded Knee military awards, which they refer to as "Medals of Dis-Honor." In commemorating the centennial of the Wounded Knee conflict in 1990, the U.S. Congress issued a statement of "deep regret" for the events that took place a century earlier, but stopped short of offering a formal apology.

The official U.S. Army flag, displayed and paraded at ceremonial events at the White House and at military posts throughout the world, has 170 streamers. Each streamer commemorates a great battle in which the U.S. Army participated. To this day, one of these streamers has stamped upon it the words "Pine Ridge 1890–1891." The conflict at Wounded Knee is described as a "battle" or "serious clash" in the U.S. Army's official records. Native Americans, however, describe it as a "massacre," and that is how it is most commonly described and understood today.

The stillness on the frozen field at Wounded Knee has long symbolized the bitter end of the unsuccessful war of Native Americans to resist control by the U.S. government. For the Sioux, in particular, the scene represented the final tragic episode in their long struggle to protect their culture, territory, and way of life, a war in which the high point had been their victory at Little Bighorn.

Although the Wounded Knee field is a fitting symbol of the end of an era, it was not in fact the end point of either the conflict or the Ghost Dance. Neither did it mark the end of the Sioux Nation as a distinct people and culture. The fighting continued for several more days as Lakota warriors attacked U.S. Army units in scattered locations. It ended on January 15, 1891, when the Ghost Dance leader Kicking Bear symbolically placed his rifle at the feet of General Miles, who accepted the surrender of the last fighters.

The Ghost Dance movement was dealt a devastating blow by the events at Wounded Knee and the failure of Wovoka's and Kicking Bear's predictions to come true in 1891. Some tribes, however, continued to practice its rituals into the early twentieth century. Wovoka remained an influential spiritual leader until his death in 1932.

As much as it symbolized the end of a long struggle, Wounded Knee also signaled the beginning of a new era of tension. The slaughter of women and children on that field poisoned relationships between the Sioux and Euro-Americans for many generations.

Tribal elders who remembered the glory days of the warrior culture of the Little Bighorn era began to realize that Wounded Knee took away more than just the lives of their fellow tribal members. The Oglala medicine man Black Elk, who took his first scalp as a 13-year-old boy at the Little Bighorn battle, was hit by the soldiers' fire at Wounded Knee. Reflecting on the massacre much later in his life, he recalled:

> I did not know how much was ended. As I look back from the high hill of my old age . . . I can see that something else died there in the bloody mud and was covered up by the blizzard. A people's dream died there. It was a beautiful dream. . . . [Now] the nation's hoop is broken and scattered. There is no center any longer, and the sacred tree is dead.[33]

The Legacy of
Little Bighorn

THE BATTLE OF THE LITTLE BIGHORN HAS ENDURED IN American popular culture, both as a widely recognized historical event and as an important symbol. This has been due primarily to the continued public fascination with the persona of George Armstrong Custer and the mystery surrounding the final fight on Last Stand Hill. Broad interest in Native American perspectives on the battle and in the meaning tribal members attached to the victory has been a comparatively recent development.

THE IMAGE AND SYMBOLISM OF CUSTER'S HEROISM IN DEFEAT

Custer was already something of a national military hero before the centennial campaign of 1876. His electrifying cavalry charges during the Civil War were well publicized. They earned him a field promotion to the rank of brigadier general at age 23, at which time he became widely known as "the Boy General." The media of the time (newspaper and magazine reporters) recognized him as a rising star. His dashing exploits,

youth, blond curls, and outlandish uniforms with red neck-
ties made for excellent stories in their publications. Custer
carefully cultivated and dearly relished his public image. He
fully realized the value it held for furthering his career.

News of the death of Custer and the defeat of his unit
began the transformation of his image from heroic to legendary. The Little Bighorn battle was one of the biggest news
stories of its era. Correspondents covering the story chose
to portray it as a tale of heroic death. In the flowery prose of
the day, they wrote vivid accounts without knowing the facts
on the ground. An article in the *New York Herald* provides a
typical example:

> In that mad charge up the narrow ravine, with the rocks
> above raining down lead upon the fated three hundred,
> with fire sprouting from every bush ahead, with the wild
> swarming horsemen circling along the heights like shriek-
> ing vultures waiting for the moment to sweep down and
> finish the bloody tale, every form, from private to general,
> rises to heroic size and the scene fixes indelibly upon the
> mind. "The Seventh fought like tigers," says the dispatch;
> yea, they died as grandly as Homer's demigods. In the su-
> preme moment of carnage, as death's relentless sweep gath-
> ered in the entire command, all distinctions of name and
> rank were blended, but the family "that died at the head of
> their column" [the Custer brothers and relatives] will lead
> the throng when history recalls their deed. . . . Success was
> beyond their grasp, so they died—to a man.[34]

Readers will quickly detect the historical inaccuracies
of this account, including the small details that there was
no general present and death had not "gathered in" the entire command.

The general theme that evolved was that Custer and his
men were tragic heroes and the Native American victors were

savage villains. A few prominent political and military leaders, including Colonel Nelson A. Miles, stated publicly that Custer was responsible for his own demise. "I regard Custer's Massacre as a sacrifice of troops," said President Ulysses Grant, "brought on by Custer himself, that was wholly unnecessary."[35] Critics, however, could not dislodge the impression in the public mind that Custer both entered the battle and died in it as a hero. The early newspaper accounts were soon reinforced by dime novels and other "pulp" publications. Within weeks of the battle, five dime novels portraying the death of the "Boy General" were released to the public. These publications were not unlike today's supermarket tabloids that seek to reveal the personal lives of Hollywood celebrities. Just six months after the battle, Frederick Whittaker rushed forth with Custer's first biography, *Life with Custer*. Filled with many falsehoods, this work served as a primary source for adventure writers for many years.

Custer's wife, Elizabeth Clift Bacon "Libbie" Custer, played a prominent role in preserving the heroic image of her late husband. Her public image was also a tragic one: a dedicated and loving spouse left widowed and childless at age 34. She took advantage of her persona to keep negative information from being made public, such as the nature of her husband's actual wounds. She worked closely with Whittaker and others who wrote favorably about Custer. Libbie also wrote three books—*Boots and Saddles, Or Life in Dakota with General Custer* (1885); *Tenting on the Plains* (1890); and *Following the Guidon* (1893)—that portrayed Custer as a loving husband, a gallant soldier, and a worthy role model. Her publications and appearances brought her both celebrity and a comfortable lifestyle. She spent her final years in an upscale apartment in New York City.

Some observers became more critical of Custer after an 1879 court of inquiry exonerated Major Marcus Reno of any wrongdoing related to the Little Bighorn battle. Critics

Elizabeth Clift Bacon "Libbie" Custer, who is pictured here with her husband in the early 1860s, did her best to preserve Custer's heroic image after his death. To help keep his image intact, Libbie wrote three books that portrayed him as a loving husband, a gallant soldier, and a worthy role model.

looked for someone else to blame besides the Native American warriors, and so turned to Custer. Still, they hardly made a dent in his positive public image. Libbie foiled most of the critics of the day by merely outliving them. She continued her campaign for Custer's heroic memory until her death in 1933, just short of her ninety-first birthday.

The story of the Little Bighorn battle with Custer as hero was not only the frequent subject of prose, but also a popular theme of poetry, art, and drama. More than 150 poems were penned about Custer's last battle. Among these were verses authored by some of America's most prominent poets, including Walt Whitman, John Greenleaf Whittier, and Henry Wadsworth Longfellow. Longfellow's 1878 poem "The Revenge of Rain-in-the-Face" perpetuated the widely held myth that the Hunkpapa warrior cut out Custer's heart as an act of revenge:

> But the foemen fled in the night,
> And Rain-in-the-Face, in his flight
> Uplifted high in air
> As a ghastly trophy, bore
> The brave heart, that beat no more,
> Of the White Chief with yellow hair.[36]

Longfellow did not reference the specific deed for which Rain in the Face sought revenge. The variations of the myth stem from the facts that, first, Tom Custer once held Rain in the Face prisoner; and, second, the younger Custer's body was found badly mutilated on Last Stand Hill. In 1905, however, Rain in the Face told Charles Eastman, the Wahpeton Dakota Sioux physician and author who had earned a medical degree at Boston University, that in the fury of battle the warriors had not personally recognized the Custers:

> Many lies have been told of me. Some say that I killed the
> Chief, and others that I cut out the heart of his brother,

because he had caused me to be imprisoned. Why, in that
fight the excitement was so great that we scarcely recognized our nearest friends.[37]

The Little Bighorn battle proved also to be an irresist-
ible theme for artists and illustrators. The collective works
of their brushes and pens could fill several museums. Nearly
2,000 artistic depictions of the battle are known to exist.
These range from oil paintings on huge canvasses to "pop
art" prints designed for mass advertising. The most famous
depiction is the so-called Adams-Becker painting entitled
Custer's Last Fight. Artist Cassilly Adams of St. Louis painted
the original work, a giant composition 9 by 16 feet, for a
traveling exhibition sometime before 1886. When the tour
failed, a local saloonkeeper purchased the oil painting to display in his bar. The tavern went bankrupt after the owner
died and the painting was acquired by one of his creditors,
the Anheuser-Busch Brewing Company, the makers of Bud-
weiser beer.

In 1895, the brewery hired E. Otto Becker to produce a
color lithograph based on the Adams painting to serve as an
advertising poster. Over the years, more than a million cop-
ies were printed, many of which were used to decorate bar
rooms around the world for generations. This led one historian to observe in 1946 that *Custer's Last Fight* "has been
viewed by a greater number of the lower-browed members of
society—and by fewer art critics—than any other picture in
American history."[38]

Adams's original painting was destroyed in a 1946 fire,
but reproductions and variations of the Becker print continue to be widely available for purchase.

One of the better paintings of the battle is Edgar S. Paxson's *Custer's Last Stand.* Paxson researched his painting for
20 years and interviewed participants of the battle on both
sides, including the warriors Gall and Two Moon. Completed

Chief Red Horse was among the Native American participants who later created pictographs of the Battle of the Little Bighorn. In this 1881 pictograph, Red Horse shows Sioux warriors who have been killed by the 7th Cavalry during the battle.

in 1900, his painting portrays 36 of the actual cavalrymen believed to have fought on Last Stand Hill, which he based on earlier photographs. The painting is now in the collection of the Buffalo Bill Historical Center in Cody, Wyoming.

Numerous Native Americans, including many battle participants, created pictographs of their interpretations of the Little Bighorn fight. They include Kicking Bear, Red Horse, Joseph White Bull, and Amos Bad Heart Bull among the Sioux, and High Bull, White Bird, and Wooden Leg among the Northern Cheyenne. Many of these pictographs are now in museum collections, although most are not on public display. One of the best pictograph series, by the Minneconjou artist Red Horse, can be viewed by appointment at the Smithsonian Institution's National Anthropological Archives in Suitland, Maryland.

In the dramatic arts, there were some stage productions based on Little Bighorn themes, but not many after the development of motion pictures. In the latter years of the nineteenth century, Custer themes became an integral part of the "Wild West" shows staged by Buffalo Bill Cody and others under the shelter of giant tents. Circus entrepreneur Adam Forepaugh was the first to incorporate a Wild West show into the standard circus format. Forepaugh's show featured a reenactment of "Custer's Last Rally" as its grand climax.

By the end of the nineteenth century, much of what the public understood about the Battle of the Little Bighorn was based on falsehoods generated by the continuing need and desire to perceive Custer as a hero. The story as legend and myth was extended when it became a popular theme of the early motion picture industry. Five full-length films on the Custer theme were produced between 1909 and 1913, including one directed by D. W. Griffith, the premier silent filmmaker. The most infamous of these early films in terms of its negative images of Native Americans was *Custer's Last Raid* (1912). Directed by Francis Ford, the older brother of

John Ford (who became famous as a director of Hollywood westerns), this movie portrayed Sitting Bull as a coward and Rain in the Face as Custer's chief nemesis.

The 1920s witnessed a further outpouring of prose and film featuring Little Bighorn as the backdrop of Custer's heroism. This was especially the case during the battle's fiftieth anniversary observance in 1926.

THE IMAGE AND SYMBOLISM OF CUSTER AS ANTIHERO

Throughout the 1920s, Custer's image remained that of "the hero of every boy." That image began to change during the beginning of the Great Depression, in the early years of the 1930s, as more of the image's promoters died off, including Libbie Custer and many of the old soldiers of the Native American wars. An intellectual style known as "debunking" came into fashion, which challenged the established views on almost everything.

Revisionist historians and other writers soon set their sites on the Custer myth. In a 1934 biography of Custer entitled *Glory Hunter*, Frederic F. Van de Water portrayed his subject as a perpetual adolescent who was overly ambitious, arrogant, brutal, detestable, incompetent, reckless, tyrannical, and vain. The University of Nebraska Press has recently republished this classic work, which sprouted the seeds of the now-prevailing image of Custer as an antihero.

Beginning in the 1920s, a physician named Thomas B. Marquis became fascinated with the idea of learning the history of the Little Bighorn battle from a Native American perspective. He began interviewing Sioux, Cheyenne, and Crow veterans of the fight. Dr. Marquis subsequently published three books based on the information imparted to him by the surviving warriors. These excellent works helped change the general public's view of both the battle and its Native American participants. In 1931, the University of Nebraska Press published Marquis's *Wooden Leg, a Warrior Who Fought Custer*. An edition of this work is still in print.

The image of the Little Bighorn battle began to change on canvas as well. In William Robinson Leigh's 1939 painting *Custer's Last Stand*, it is the Native American warriors who are portrayed as heroic and Custer and his troops are merely presented as dim figures in the background obscured by the dust and the smoke of the battle. This work can be viewed at the Woolaroc Museum in Bartlesville, Oklahoma.

Despite the debunking in print and in some paintings, the heroic Custer image continued to prevail in films. This was particularly evident in Warner Brothers studio's 1941 spectacle *They Died with Their Boots On*. With Errol Flynn playing a swashbuckling Custer and Olivia de Havilland as his loving Libbie, this film perpetuated almost every cliché of the nineteenth-century Custer legend. In this version of the story, it is Crazy Horse, and not Rain in the Face, who gets his revenge on Custer for an earlier capture. Released at a time when World War II was threatening to involve the United States, the not-so-hidden agenda of the film's script was to promote an image of American patriotism and courage. For example, when Libbie begs her husband not to go off to battle in Montana, Custer replies, "I must go. It is my duty. I'm an officer in the United States Army." *They Died with Their Boots On* is now available in DVD video format. Viewing it provides an excellent means of quickly gaining an understanding of the enduring Custer mythology.

In the twentieth century, Custer evolved beyond his legend to also become a universal symbol. Because of its instant and wide recognition, the mere name "Custer" could stand for whatever character traits anyone wanted to assign to his image. For most of the century following the Little Bighorn battle, Custer's prevailing symbolism was that of heroic traits. However, he also became a metaphor for the lost cause, abandoned hope, and looming disaster in whatever context anyone chose to reference his name. His symbolism became a part of admonishing speeches, editorial comments, political cartoons, and the jokes of comedians.

THE IMAGE AND SYMBOLISM OF NATIVE AMERICAN PRIDE

By the 1960s, a darker image was attached to Custer as he came to symbolize all of his country's misdeeds against Native Americans. In 1968, Sioux author Vine Deloria Jr. helped launch a protest movement with his best-selling book *Custer Died for Your Sins*. Native American activists picked up this symbolism and proudly displayed bumper stickers that proclaimed, "Custer Had It Coming."

Deloria's book also revealed to the general public that Custer had long been the most popular subject of derisive humor among Native Americans. "There are probably more jokes about Custer and the Indians," he wrote, "than there were participants in the battle." The following is a good, short example: "When Custer left for Montana he told the Bureau of Indian Affairs not to do anything until he returned . . . and it hasn't."

According to Deloria, the reason that Custer has become such a universal punch line among native people is that "[all] tribes, even those thousands of miles from Montana, feel a sense of accomplishment when thinking of Custer. Custer binds together implacable foes because he represented the Ugly American of the last century, and he got what was coming to him."

Following in the footsteps of Thomas B. Marquis, other history buffs sought out Native American interpretations of the Little Bighorn battle. In 1957, for example, portrait artist David Humphreys Miller published *Custer's Fall: The Indian Side of the Story*. This book is still available from used and rare book dealers.

In the 1960s, films also began more often to view Native Americans as human beings and not just pesky, impersonal objects in the way of soldiers and cowboys. These films increasingly portrayed Custer as a bloodthirsty destroyer of Native American families. The outstanding example of this genre is the 1970 film *Little Big Man*, which director Arthur Penn adapted to the screen from Thomas Berger's novel of the same name. In common with *They Died with Their Boots On*, this movie also used Custer to make a statement about an ongoing war. Only this time, Custer symbolized barbarism rather than heroism. Actor Richard Mulligan played him as a lunatic, insanely raging about the battlefield, shouting incoherently. This image served as a metaphor of the barbarism of the United States in the Native American wars of the nineteenth century and in the Vietnam War that was raging at the time of the film's release. *Little Big Man*, in which actor Dustin Hoffman plays the 111-year-old Cheyenne narrator of the story, is readily available in DVD format. Berger's novel is also still in print.

In total, Custer's character has been featured in more than 70 film and television productions. In comparison, Crazy Horse has only been portrayed 13 times on film and Sitting Bull only 11 times. By the 1990s, Custer's image was so fluid on film that he was portrayed as the all-American, spirited West Point cadet in the made-for-television production *Class of '61* (1993) at the same time that he was frequently vilified in the mode of the *Little Big Man* image in the TV drama series *Dr. Quinn, Medicine Woman*.

The Battle of the Little Bighorn has received much less attention in popular music. The first and probably worst pop song on the theme was Larry Verne's *Mister Custer*, which made the Billboard Top 10 in 1961. In the song, an enlisted cavalryman has a dream about an impending disaster and pleads with the commander to be dismissed. *Mister Custer* was extremely derogatory toward the Native American warriors, referring to them as "injuns" and "redskins" and making a lame joke about them "running around like a bunch of wild Indians."[39] The wide popularity of its base attempt at humor demonstrated that negative stereotypes of Native Americans were still widely held.

In 1964, country singer Johnny Cash provided a different perspective in a song called "Custer" that he featured on *Bitter Tears*, an album that focused exclusively on Native American history and problems. Cash was then convinced that he had Cherokee ancestry and this helped inspire the recording, though he later found that he in fact had no Cherokee blood. Cash also referenced Crazy Horse, Sitting Bull, and Gall, and said of Custer in an earlier verse: "With victories he was swimmin' he killed children dogs and women."

More recent recordings have continued the theme of mocking Custer and questioning the heroism of his defeat at Little Bighorn. These include "The Punch Line" by the punk/alternative band The Minutemen on their 1981 album of the same name; "Little Big Horn" by the German heavy metal band Running Wild on their 1991 album, *Blazon Stone*; "History Is Made by Stupid People" by the Canadian musical comedy group The Arrogant Worms on their 1995 album, *C'est Cheese*; and "Custer Died A-Runnin" by Canadian singer David Wilkie on his 1996 album, *Cowboy Celtic*.

Enthusiasts of tactical and strategic war gaming can play out the Battle of the Little Bighorn on a limited number of board or computer games. The latest board game is *Battle of Little Bighorn* (Khyber Pass Games, 2005). One of the few readily available computer simulations is *Custer's Last Command 2: The Battle of the Little Bighorn* (Incredible Simulations, Inc., 1995).

As the bibliography of this book reflects in small part, the Battle of the Little Bighorn has been the subject of hundreds of publications. It is probably the most studied subject in the history of the American West, in addition to being one

In 1991, the U.S. Congress changed the name of Custer Battlefield National Monument to Little Bighorn Battlefield National Monument. To further honor the Native American participants in the battle, the National Park Service unveiled its Indian memorial at Little Bighorn Battlefield during the one-hundred-twenty-seventh anniversary of the battle on June 25, 2003.

of the most researched battles in the military history of the world. The two most significant developments in this scholarship since the 1980s have been the findings of archeological investigations of Last Stand Hill and the integration of this data with a more careful study of the existing testimony of Native American participants of the battle. The two best works resulting from this research are Richard Alan Fox Jr.'s *Archeology, History and Custer's Last Battle* (1993) and Gregory F. Michno's *Lakota Noon: The Indian Narrative of Custer's Defeat* (1997).

The most relevant way to learn more about the Battle of the Little Bighorn is to visit the site in southeastern Montana where it took place. The National Park Service has preserved two parcels of land along the Little Bighorn River as the Little Bighorn National Battlefield Monument. The visitor's center does an excellent job of providing orientation to the battlefield. For further information about the monument, visit its Web site at *www.nps.gov/libi*. The fact that its official name was changed from Custer Battlefield in 1991 reflects the gradual change in the national consciousness about the history and significance of the battle.

The Battle of the Little Bighorn will continue to be an important event in American history for as long as people remain intrigued by its mysteries and the personalities of its participants. Its importance will also endure for as long as historians, students, and readers continue to find meaning and purpose in whatever factual or symbolic significance they assign to it.

Chronology

1685 Sioux groups move west from Minnesota.

1707 Sioux begin trading for horses.

1806 Cheyenne and Arapaho form an alliance against the Sioux.

1826 Arapaho, Cheyenne, and Sioux form an uneasy alliance.

1851 Alliance of the Sioux, Cheyenne, and Arapaho dominates the northern and central plains; Fort Laramie Treaty establishes the

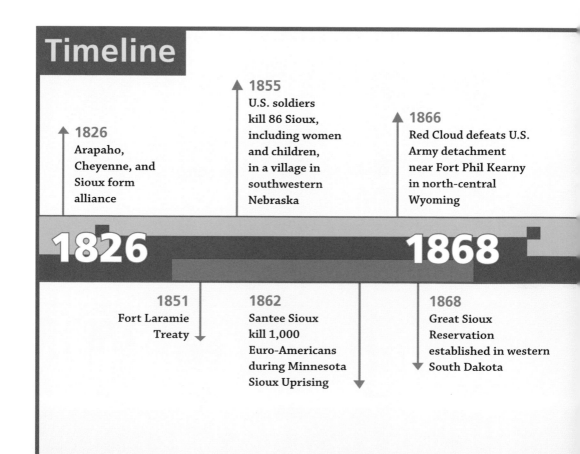

Timeline

1826
Arapaho, Cheyenne, and Sioux form alliance

1855
U.S. soldiers kill 86 Sioux, including women and children, in a village in southwestern Nebraska

1866
Red Cloud defeats U.S. Army detachment near Fort Phil Kearny in north-central Wyoming

1826

1868

1851
Fort Laramie Treaty

1862
Santee Sioux kill 1,000 Euro-Americans during Minnesota Sioux Uprising

1868
Great Sioux Reservation established in western South Dakota

boundaries of the aforementioned tribes' territory (in addition to that of the Arikara, Assiniboine, Crow, Hidatsa, Mandan, and Shoshone), and the tribes pledge that they won't engage in war against one another.

Early 1850s Settlers traveling along the Oregon Trail have several run-ins with the Sioux in what is today Nebraska and Wyoming.

1854 Sioux war party kills three people on a mail wagon along the Oregon Trail.

1855 U.S. soldiers under the command of Brigadier General William S. Harney attack a Sioux village in southwestern Nebraska, killing

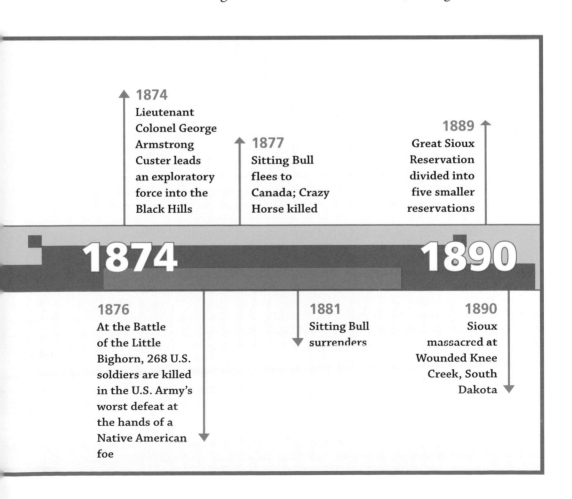

1874
Lieutenant Colonel George Armstrong Custer leads an exploratory force into the Black Hills

1877
Sitting Bull flees to Canada; Crazy Horse killed

1889
Great Sioux Reservation divided into five smaller reservations

1874   **1890**

1876
At the Battle of the Little Bighorn, 268 U.S. soldiers are killed in the U.S. Army's worst defeat at the hands of a Native American foe

1881
Sitting Bull surrenders

1890
Sioux massacred at Wounded Knee Creek, South Dakota

86 people, including women and children; for the first time, the Sioux are privy to the brutality of the U.S. Army.

1856 Sioux agree not to attack other tribes or Euro-Americans crossing their territory.

1861–1865 U.S. Civil War.

1862 Bear Ribs assassinated for accepting annuity goods from the U.S. government; during the Minnesota Sioux Uprising, Santee Sioux kill 1,000 Euro-Americans, including 23 infantrymen of the U.S. Army.

1863 U.S. Army launches retaliatory campaign against the Santee Sioux; over the next 18 years, the U.S. Army and the Sioux will be in a perpetual state of warfare; in September, General Alfred Sully defeats coalition of Nakota, Dakota, and Lakota Sioux warriors at Whitestone Hill in southeastern North Dakota.

1864 In July, Sully defeats Sioux coalition in the Killdeer Mountains of western North Dakota.

1866 Red Cloud and his warriors soundly defeat a U.S. Army detachment under the command of Captain William J. Fetterman near Fort Phil Kearny in north-central Wyoming.

1866–68 After gold is discovered in Montana, Sioux war parties disrupt travelers along Bozeman trail.

1867 U.S. Army defeats Sioux at the Wagon Box in north-central Wyoming and the Hayfield fight in south-central Montana.

1868 Under the terms of the Fort Laramie Treaty of 1868, the U.S. government establishes the Great Sioux Reservation in western South Dakota.

1869–74 Size of U.S. Army cut in half.

1870 By this year, Sitting Bull has become one of the primary leaders among the Sioux.

1874 Lieutenant Colonel George Armstrong Custer leads an exploratory force of 1,000 troops to the Black Hills of South Dakota.

1875 On December 6, Office of Indian Affairs orders all Sioux to return to the reservation by January 31, 1876.

1876 In spring, generals Alfred H. Terry and George Crook launch campaign against "hostiles" who refuse to return to the reservation.

MAY U.S. forces under the command of Colonel John Gibbons head east from Fort Shaw and Fort Ellis in Montana, while General Terry moves west from Fort Abraham Lincoln in present-day North Dakota, and General Crook moves north from Fort Fetterman in Wyoming.

EARLY JUNE Large group of Sioux and Northern Cheyennes gather on Rosebud Creek in Montana for their annual Sun Dance; Sitting Bull has a vision that portends future success for the Sioux.

JUNE 25 At the Battle of the Little Bighorn, 268 U.S. soldiers are killed in the U.S. Army's worst defeat at the hands of a Native American foe.

SEPTEMBER General Crook defeats Sioux near Slim Buttes (South Dakota) and burns American Horse's village.

OCTOBER Colonel Nelson Miles forces the surrender of 2,000 Minneconjou and Sans Arc Sioux in Montana.

1877 Sioux forced to give up their sacred grounds in Black Hills; in May, Sitting Bull flees to Canada; in September, Crazy Horse killed at Camp Robinson, Nebraska.

1881 Sitting Bull and his remaining followers surrender at Fort Buford on the Missouri River in present-day North Dakota.

1889 U.S. government divides Great Sioux
Reservation into five smaller reservations:
Cheyenne River, Lower Brulé, Pine Ridge,
Rosebud, and Standing Rock.

1890 On December 29, as many as 300 of Big
Foot's band of Lakota are massacred by the
U.S. Army at Wounded Knee Creek, South
Dakota.

Notes

Chapter 4

1. John S. Gray, *Centennial Campaign: The Sioux War of 1876* (Norman: University of Oklahoma Press, 1988), 147.
2. Peter Panzieri, *Little Big Horn 1876: Custer's Last Stand*, Osprey Military Classic Battles Series, (London: Reed International Books Ltd., 1997), 44.

Chapter 5

3. Panzieri, *Little Big Horn 1876*, 49.
4. Evan S. Connell, *Son of the Morning Star: Custer and The Little Bighorn* (New York: North Point Press, 1984), 274.
5. Panzieri, *Little Big Horn 1876*, 51.
6. Gregory F. Michno, *Lakota Noon: The Indian Narrative of Custer's Defeat* (Missoula, Mont.: Mountain Press Publishing Company, 1997), 39.

Chapter 6

7. Michno, *Lakota Noon*, 39.
8. Ibid., 41.
9. Thom Hatch, *The Custer Companion: A Comprehensive Guide to the Life of George Armstrong: Custer and the Plains Indian Wars* (Mechanicsburg, Pa.: Stackpole Books, 2001), 211.

10. Panzieri, *Little Big Horn 1876*, 56.
11. Ibid., 60.
12. Thom Hatch, *Custer and the Battle of the Little Bighorn: An Encyclopedia* (Jefferson, N.C.: McFarland & Company, Inc., Publishers, 1997), 155.
13. Panzieri, *Little Big Horn 1876*, 61.

Chapter 7

14. Richard A. Fox Jr., *Archeology, History, and Custer's Last Battle: The Little Big Horn Reexamined* (Norman: University of Oklahoma Press, 1993), 147.
15. Ibid.

Chapter 8

16. Michno, *Lakota Noon*, 195.
17. Ibid., 212.
18. Ibid., 216.
19. Richard G. Hardorff, compiler and editor, *Lakota Recollections of the Custer Fight: New Sources of Indian Military History* (Lincoln: University of Nebraska Press, 1991), 189.
20. Richard G. Hardorff, compiler and editor, *Cheyenne Memories of the Custer Fight* (Lincoln: University of Nebraska Press, 1995), 36.
21. Michno, *Lakota Noon*, 276.
22. Ibid., 259.

23. Herman J. Viola, *The Little Bighorn Remembered: The Untold Story of Custer's Last Stand* (New York: Times Books, 1999), 53.

24. Panzieri, *Little Big Horn 1876*, 82.

Chapter 9

25. Robert M. Utley, *The Lance and the Shield: The Life and Times of Sitting Bull* (New York: Henry Holt and Co., 1993), 232.

26. Ibid., 269.

27. Robert M. Utley, *The Last Days of the Sioux Nation* (Second edition) (New Haven, Conn.: Yale University Press, 2004), 70.

28. Utley, *The Lance and the Shield*, 302.

29. Utley, *The Last Days of the Sioux Nation*, 193.

30. Dee Brown, *Bury My Heart at Wounded Knee: An Indian History of the American West* (New York: Henry Holt, 2001), 444.

31. Utley, *The Last Days of the Sioux Nation*, 217.

32. Rex Alan Smith, *Moon of the Popping Trees: The Tragedy at Wounded Knee and the End of the Indian Wars* (Lincoln: University of Nebraska Press, 1981), 203.

33. Ibid., 199–200.

Chapter 10

34. Robert M. Utley, *Cavalier in Buckskin: George Armstrong Custer and the Western Military Frontier* (Norman: University of Oklahoma Press, 1988), 11.

35. Ibid.

36. Ibid., 12. The full text of this poem can be found at *http://www.everypoet. com/archive/poetry/Henry_ Wadsworth_Longfellow/ longfellow_birds_of_passage_ the_revenge_of_rain_in_the_ face.htm.*

37. Louise Barnett, *Touched by Fire: The Life, Death and Mythic Afterlife of George Armstrong Custer* (Lincoln: University of Nebraska Press, 2006), 400.

38. Robert Taft, "The Pictorial Record of the Old West. IV. Custer's Last Stand. John Mulvany, Cassilly Adams and Otto Becker," *Kansas Historical Quarterly* XIV: 4 (Winter 1946), 362.

39. "Mr. Custer" sung by Larry Verne, words and music by Fred Darian, Al DeLory, and Joe Van Winkle, 1960. The full lyrics to this song can be found at *http://canciones.astalaweb. com/Venglish/resultados. asp?param=Canciones/L/ Larry_Verne—Mr_custer.txt.*

Bibliography

Ambrose, Stephen E. *Crazy Horse and Custer: The Parallel Lives of Two American Warriors*. New York: Anchor Books, 1996.

Barnett, Louise. *Touched by Fire: The Life, Death and Mythic Afterlife of George Armstrong Custer*. Lincoln: University of Nebraska Press, 2006.

Bray, Kingsley M. *Crazy Horse: A Lakota Life*. Norman: University of Oklahoma Press, 2006.

Brown, Dee. *Bury My Heart at Wounded Knee: An Indian History of the American West*. New York: Henry Holt, 2001.

Coleman, William S. E. *Voices of Wounded Knee*. Lincoln: University of Nebraska Press, 2000.

Connell, Evan S. *Son of the Morning Star: Custer and The Little Bighorn*. New York: North Point Press, 1984.

Day, Carl F. *Tom Custer: Ride to Glory*. Norman: University of Oklahoma Press, 2005.

Deloria, Vine, Jr. *Custer Died for Your Sins: An Indian Manifesto*. Norman: University of Oklahoma Press, 1988.

DeMallie, Raymond J. "Teton." In *Handbook of North American Indians*, vol. 13, pt. 2, *Plains*. Washington, D.C.: Smithsonian Institution Press, 2001, pp. 794–820; "Yankton and Yanktonai." In *Handbook of North American Indians*, vol. 13, pt. 2, *Plains*. Washington, D.C.: Smithsonian Institution Press, 2001, pp. 777–993.

Dippie, Brian W. *Custer's Last Stand: An Anatomy of an American Myth*. Lincoln: University of Nebraska Press, 1994.

Fox, Richard A., Jr. *Archeology, History, and Custer's Last Battle: The Little Big Horn Reexamined*. Norman: University of Oklahoma Press, 1993.

Fowler, Loretta. "Arapaho." In *Handbook of North American Indians*, vol. 13, pt. 2, *Plains*. Washington, D.C.: Smithsonian Institution Press, 2001, pp. 840–862.

———. "History of the United States Plains Since 1850." In *Handbook of North American Indians*, vol. 13, pt. 1, *Plains*. Washington, D.C.: Smithsonian Institution Press, 2001, pp. 280–299.

Frost, Lawrence A. *The Custer Album: A Pictorial Biography of George Armstrong Custer*. Norman: University of Oklahoma Press, 1990.

Gray, John S. *Centennial Campaign: The Sioux War of 1876*. Norman: University of Oklahoma Press, 1988.

———. *Custer's Last Campaign: Mitch Boyer and the Little Big Horn Reconstructed*. Lincoln: University of Nebraska Press, 1991.

Greene, Jerome E., comp., ed., ann., *Battles and Skirmishes of the Great Sioux War, 1876–1877: The Military View*. Lincoln: University of Nebraska Press, 1993.

———. *Lakota and Cheyenne: Indian Views of the Great Sioux War, 1876–1877*. Norman: University of Oklahoma Press, 1994.

Hammer, Kenneth M. *Custer in '76: Walter Camp's Notes on the Custer Fight*. Norman: University of Oklahoma Press, 1990.

Hardorff, Richard G. *Hokahey! A Good Day to Die: The Indian Casualties of the Custer Fight*. Spokane, Wash.: Arthur H. Clark, 1991.

———, comp. and ed. *Cheyenne Memories of the Custer Fight*. Lincoln: University of Nebraska Press, 1995.

———, comp. and ed. *Indian Views of the Custer Fight: A Source Book*. Norman: University of Oklahoma Press, 2006.

———, comp. and ed. *Lakota Recollections of the Custer Fight: New Sources of Indian Military History*. Lincoln: University of Nebraska Press, 1991.

Hassrick, Royal B. *The Sioux: Life and Times of a Warrior Society*. Norman: University of Oklahoma Press, 1964.

Hatch, Thom. *Custer and the Battle of the Little Bighorn: An Encyclopedia*. Jefferson, N.C.: McFarland & Company, Publishers, 1997.

———. *The Custer Companion: A Comprehensive Guide to the Life of George Armstrong Custer and the Plains Indian Wars*. Mechanicsburg, Pa.: Stackpole Books, 2001.

Hedren, Paul L. *We Trailed the Sioux: Enlisted Men Speak on Custer, Crook, and the Great Sioux War*. Mechanicsburg, Pa.: Stackpole Books, 2003.

Hutton, Paul Andrew, ed. *The Custer Reader*. Lincoln: University of Nebraska Press, 1992.

Michno, Gregory F. *Lakota Noon: The Indian Narrative of Custer's Defeat*. Missoula, Mont.: Mountain Press Publishing Company, 1997.

Mooney, James. *The Ghost Dance Religion and the Sioux Outbreak of 1890*. Lincoln: University of Nebraska Press, 1994.

Moore, John. H., Margot P. Liberty, and A. Terry Straus. "Cheyenne." In *Handbook of North American Indians*, vol. 13, pt. 2, *Plains*. Washington, D.C.: Smithsonian Institution Press, 2001, pp. 863–885.

Neihardt, John G. *Black Elk Speaks*. Lincoln: University of Nebraska Press, 2004.

Panzieri, Peter. *Little Big Horn 1876: Custer's Last Stand*. Osprey Military Classic Battles Series. London: Reed International Books, 1997.

Scott, Douglas D., and Richard A. Fox Jr. *Archaeological Insights into the Custer Battle: An Assessment of the 1984 Field Season*. Norman: University of Oklahoma Press, 1987.

———, Richard A. Fox Jr., Melissa A. Conner, and Dick Harmon. *Archeological Perspectives on the Battle of the Little Big Horn*. Norman: University of Oklahoma Press, 1989.

———, Melissa A. Connor, and P. Willey. *They Died with Custer: Soldiers' Bones from the Battle of the Little Bighorn*. Norman: University of Oklahoma Press, 2002.

Sklenar, Larry. *To Hell with Honor: Custer and the Little Bighorn*. Norman: University of Oklahoma Press, 2000.

Smith, Rex Alan. *Moon of the Popping Trees: The Tragedy at Wounded Knee and the End of the Indian Wars*. Lincoln: University of Nebraska Press, 1981.

Stewart, Edgar I. *Custer's Luck*. Norman: University of Oklahoma Press, 1980.

Taft, Robert. "The Pictorial Record of the Old West. IV. Custer's Last Stand. John Mulvany, Cassilly Adams and Otto Becker." *Kansas Historical Quarterly* XIV: 4 (Winter 1946), p. 362.

Utley, Robert M. *Cavalier in Buckskin: George Armstrong Custer and the Western Military Frontier*. Norman: University of Oklahoma Press, 1988.

——. *Custer and the Great Controversy: The Origin and Development of a Legend*. Lincoln: University of Nebraska Press, 1998.

——. *Frontier Regulars: The United States Army and the Indian, 1866–1891*. Lincoln: University of Nebraska Press, 1984.

——. *Frontiersmen in Blue: The United States Army and The Indian, 1848–1865*. Lincoln: University of Nebraska Press, 1981.

——. *The Lance and the Shield: The Life and Times of Sitting Bull*. New York: Henry Holt, 1993.

——. *Little Bighorn Battlefield: A History and Guide to The Battle of the Little Bighorn*. U.S. Department of the Interior, National Park Service, Division of Publications. Washington, D.C.: Government Printing Office, 1994.

——. *The Last Days of the Sioux Nation* (Second edition). New Haven, Conn.: Yale University Press, 2004.

Van de Water, Frederic F. *Glory Hunter: A Life of General Custer*. Reprint of 1934 edition. Lincoln: University of Nebraska Press, 1988.

Viola, Herman J., with Jan Shelton Danis. *It Is a Good Day to Die: Indian Eyewitnesses Tell the Story of the Battle of the Little Bighorn*. Lincoln: University of Nebraska Press, 1998.

——. *The Little Bighorn Remembered: The Untold Story of Custer's Last Stand*. New York: Times Books, 1999.

Walker, James R. *Lakota Society*. Edited by Raymond J. DeMallie. Lincoln: University of Nebraska Press, 1992.

White, Richard. "The Winning of the West: The Expansion of the Western Sioux in the Eighteenth and Nineteenth Centuries." In *Journal of American History*. 65, 2 (1978), 319–343.

Whittaker, Frederick. *A Complete Life of General George A. Custer*. Vols. 1 and 2. Reprint of 1879 edition. Lincoln: University of Nebraska Press, 1992.

Further Reading

Barnett, Louise. *Touched by Fire: The Life, Death and Mythic Afterlife of George Armstrong Custer*. Lincoln: University of Nebraska Press, 2006.

Bray, Kingsley M. *Crazy Horse: A Lakota Life*. Norman: University of Oklahoma Press, 2006.

Brust, James S., Brian C. Pohanka, and Sandy Barnard. *Where Custer Fell: Photographs of the Little Bighorn Battlefield Then and Now*. Norman: University of Oklahoma Press, 2005.

Coleman, William S. E. *Voices of Wounded Knee*. Lincoln: University of Nebraska Press, 2000.

Custer, Elizabeth B. *Boots and Saddles, Or, Life in Dakota with General Custer*. Norman: University of Oklahoma Press, 1961.

Day, Carl F. *Tom Custer: Ride to Glory*. Norman: University of Oklahoma Press, 2005.

Fox, Richard A., Jr. *Archeology, History, and Custer's Last Battle: The Little Big Horn Reexamined*. Norman: University of Oklahoma Press, 1993.

Gray, John S. *Centennial Campaign: The Sioux War of 1876*. Norman: University of Oklahoma Press, 1988.

——. *Custer's Last Campaign: Mitch Boyer and the Little Big Horn Reconstructed*. Lincoln: University of Nebraska Press, 1991.

Hammer, Kenneth M. *Custer in '76: Walter Camp's Notes on the Custer Fight*. Norman: University of Oklahoma Press, 1990.

Leckie, Shirley A. *Elizabeth Bacon Custer and the Making of a Myth*. Norman: University of Oklahoma Press, 1993.

Marquis, Thomas B., interpreter. *Wooden Leg: A Warrior Who Fought Custer* (Second Edition). Lincoln: University of Nebraska Press, 2003.

Michno, Gregory F. *Lakota Noon: The Indian Narrative of Custer's Defeat*. Missoula, Mont.: Mountain Press Publishing Company, 1997.

Nichols, Ronald H. *In Custer's Shadow: Major Marcus Reno*. Norman: University of Oklahoma Press, 2000.

Utley, Robert M. *The Lance and the Shield: The Life and Times of Sitting Bull*. New York: Henry Holt, 1993.

WEB SITES

Black Elk Speaks: The Life Story of a Holy Man of the Oglala Sioux
http://blackelkspeaks.unl.edu/blackelk.pdf

Custer Battlefield Historical and Museum Association
www.cbhma.org

Native American View on the Wounded Knee Massacre
http://www.english.uiuc.edu/maps/poets/m_r/momaday/knee.htm

Comanche: The Seventh Cavalry's Only Survivor on Last Stand Hill
www.equinenet.org/heroes/comanche.html

Friends of the Little Bighorn Battlefield
www.friendslittlebighorn.com

Little Bighorn Associates
www.lbha.org

Little Bighorn Photo Gallery
www.mohicanpress.com/battles/ba04002.html

Wounded Knee Slide Show
http://msnbc.com/onair/msnbc/TimeandAgain/archive/wknee/1890.asp?cp1=1

The Little Bighorn Battlefield National Monument
www.nps.gov/libi/index.htm

Biography of Wovoka
http://www.pbs.org/weta/thewest/people/s_z/wovoka.htm

Bureau of American Ethnology's Report on the Ghost Dance Religion
www.pbs.org/weta/thewest/resources/archives/eight/gdmessg.htm

The Fort Laramie Treaty of 1868
www.pbs.org/weta/thewest/resources/archives/four/ftlaram.htm

An Eyewitness Account of the Little Bighorn Battle by the Lakota
Chief Red Horse
**www.pbs.org/weta/thewest/resources/archives/six/bighorn.
htm**

Wounded Knee Museum
www.woundedkneemuseum.org/

Picture Credits

page:

8: Courtesy of The Library of Congress [LC-USZ62-512]

13: Courtesy of the Library of Congress [LC-USZC4-7163]

18: Courtesy of the Library of Congress [LC-US62-107919]

25: Courtesy of the Library of Congress [LC-US62-102187]

33: National Archives Records Administration

37: © Infobase Publishing

40: Courtesy of the Library of Congress [LC-US62-111147]

47: Courtesy of the Library of Congress [LC-DIG-cwpb-05341]

53: The Granger Collection, New York

57: Denver Public Library, Western History Collection, D. F. Barry, B-539

65: The Granger Collection, New York

67: The Granger Collection, New York

71: Denver Public Library, Western History Collection, D. F. Barry, B-101

76: Denver Public Library, Western History Collection, D. F. Barry, B-543

79: Denver Public Library, Western History Collection, D. F. Barry, B-272

87: Denver Public Library, Western History Collection, X-31427

92: Copyright © North Wind/ North Wind Picture Archives

96: © Infobase Publishing

106: Courtesy of the Library of Congress [LC-USZCN4-37]

111: Courtesy of the Library of Congress [LC-USZ62-52423]

117: The Granger Collection, New York

120: Courtesy of the Library of Congress [LC-DIG-ppmc-02532]

124: National Archives Records Administration

132: Courtesy of the Library of Congress [LC-DIG-cwpbh-03130]

135: The Granger Collection, New York

142: Associated Press/Bob Zellar

Cover: The Granger Collection, New York

Index

A

Adams-Becker painting, 134
African Americans, 69
allotments, 109, 126
American Horse, 26, 104
annuity goods, 29, 32–33, 39
Antelope, 59, 60, 82, 86, 90, 99, 107
Arapahos, 14–15, 27, 28
Arikara scouts, 20–21, 58, 63, 68, 70
artwork, 134–136
Ash Hollow, Battle of, 31
Ashishishe (Curley), 71, 73

B

Badlands, 114
Bates Creek, Battle of, 105
battalions, defined, 21
Bear Coat, 83, 104–107, 113, 118,
    126, 131
Bear Ribs, 32–33
Beard, Dewey, 125, 126
Becker, E. Otto, 134
Belknap, William, 48
Benteen, Frederick, 51–52, 56, 61,
    64–66, 78
Berger, Thomas, 140
Big Foot, 77, 112, 116–124
Big Horn Mountains, 38
Big Mound, Battle of, 35–36
Big Road, 26
Bighead, Kate, 59–60, 82, 86, 90,
    99, 107
biographies, 131
Black Coyote, 122
Black Elk, 59, 128
Black Foot Band, 24, 26, 29, 32–33
Black Hawk War, 30
Black Hills, 41–42, 103–104, 108
Black Kettle, 10
Black Moon, 26
Blackfeet tribe, 13, 24
Blue Mountain, 122
Blue Water Creek, Battle of, 31
Bobtail Horse, 75

Bouyer, Minton "Mitch", 21, 72, 73
Bozeman Trail, 35, 36, 38
Brave Wolf, 97, 106
Brisbin, James, 50
Brooke, John R., 118, 119
Brotherton, David H., 108
Brulé Sioux, 23, 25, 26, 29–32
buffalo, 14, 23, 29, 69
Buffalo Bill's Wild West, 110, 136
Buffalo Lake, Battle of, 35–36
buffalo soldiers, 20
Bull Head, 114
Butler Ridge, 75, 76–77

C

Calhoun, James, 52, 79, 80–83
Canada, retreat to, 104, 107–108
Cankpe Opi Wakpala, 118
Cash, Johnny, 141
Catch the Bear, 114
celebrity, Sitting Bull as, 109–110
Cemetery Ridge, 84
Ceska Maza, 114
Cheyenne River Reservation, 109,
    113, 115–116
Cheyennes, 14–15, 18, 26, 28
Chippewa Indians, 22–23
Closed Hand, 89, 90
Collins, Mary, 110
Comes in Sight, 89
companies, defined, 21
Congressional Medal of Honor, 100,
    101, 121, 126–127
Conquering Bear, 29–30
Contrary Belly, 89
controversy, 11, 97–100
coulee, defined, 73
counting coup, 16, 24, 89
cows, 31, 32
Craft, Francis, 125
Crawler, 70
Crazy Horse
    Battle of the Rosebud
        45–46

Crazy Horse (*continued*)
    Battle of Wolf Mountain and, 105
    counterattack of, 90–91
    death of, 106, 107
    film portrayal of, 138, 140
    George Crook and, 104
    life of, 46
    Little Bighorn village and, 26
    as military genius, 11
    Powder River survivors and, 44
    Red Cloud's War and, 36
    Reno's retreat and, 66, 68
    ridge campaign of, 81–82
    surrender of, 105–106
    War of the Mormon Cow and, 31
Creek wars, 30
Crook, George, 43–46, 49, 104, 107
Crow Dog, 25, 26
Crow Foot, 114–115
Crow King, 26, 70
Crow tribe, 20–21
Crow's Nest, 54, 55, 121
Curley, 71, 73
Custer, Boston, 98
Custer, Elizabeth Clift Bacon, 131–133, 137
Custer, George Armstrong
    as antihero, 137–139
    Black Hills exploration and, 41–42
    counterattack on, 62–66
    Dakota column and, 46–48
    death of, 7, 98–99
    as hero, 129–137
    ignoring of scouts' advice and, 73
    last stand of, 11, 97–100
    offensive of, 51–58
    overview of, 9
    ridge battles of, 74–75, 78–81, 84
    7th Cavalry and, 48–49
    suspension of, 48
Custer, Margaret Emma, 80

Custer, Thomas W., 52, 55, 98, 133
Custer Battlefield National Monument, 142–143
Custer Died for Your Sins (Deloria), 139
Custer's Fall: The Indian Side of the Story (Miller), 139
Cut Belly, 89, 90

D
Dakota people, 23
Deeds, 70, 72
Deep Coulee Ford, 75, 78, 81
Deloria, Vine Jr., 139
deploying units, defined, 21
Dewey Beard, 125, 126
Died with Their Boots On, They, 98, 138, 140
diseases, Oregon Trail and, 29
Dorman, Isaiah, 69–70, 72
drunkenness, Marcus Reno and, 52
Dull Knife Fight, 105
Dunn, John "Red Beard", 116–117

E
Eagle Elk, 72
Eastman, Charles, 133–134

F
Face, Julia, 93
Fast Bull, 26
Fears Nothing, 74
Fetterman Massacre, 36–38, 46
Flying By, 109–110
Flynn, Errol, 98, 138
fords, defined, 75
Forepaugh, Adam, 136
Forsyth, James, 119–120, 123, 126
Fort Laramie, Treaty of 1851, 28–29, 32–33
Fort Laramie, Treaty of 1868, 37, 38, 39, 41
Fox, Richard A. Jr., 97–98, 142

G
Gall, 11, 26, 59–60, 91–92, 104, 134
Gatling guns, 48, 50
Gerard, Frederick F., 70–72
Geronimo, 43

Ghost Dance religion, 35, 110–116, 121–122, 127–128
Ghost Shirts, 113
Gibbons, John, 44–45, 48, 49
Glory Hunter (Van de Water), 137
Godfrey, Edward S., 123
gold, 36, 42
Goldin, Theodore, 66
Good Bear Boy, 63
Grant, Orvil, 48
Grant, Ulysses S., 43, 48, 131
Grattan, John A., 29–31
Grattan Massacre, 31, 32
Gray Horse Troop, 75, 83, 84, 86, 89–90
Greasy Grass, Battle of, 8
Great Sioux Reservation, 15, 37–38, 92, 104–106, 109
Griffith, D. W., 136
guidons, 22, 77, 95

H

Harney, William Selby, 30, 31–32
Harrison, Benjamin, 113
Hawk Man, 68
Hayfield fight, 38
He Dog, 26, 44
Henryville, 91–92
High Forehead, 30, 32
horses, 14, 17–18, 63, 85–87, 95, 119
Hotchkiss guns, 120, 123
Hump, 26, 82, 106, 116
Hunkpapa band. *See also* Sitting Bull
    Fort Laramie Treaty of 1851 and, 29, 32–33
    Little Bighorn village and, 23–24, 26
    response to Reno's attack, 62–63
    Standing Rock Agency and, 108
    Wounded Knee and, 125

I

Ice. *See* White Bull
Incredible Simulations, Inc., 141
Inkpaduta, 26
Iron Hail, 125, 126

(Ish Hayu Nishus). *See* Two Moon
isolationism, Sitting Bull and, 41

J

Jumping Bear, 26

K

Keogh, Myles W., 56–57, 77–80, 90–91, 93–95
Kicking Bear, 111, 112–114, 128
Kill Eagle, 26
Killdeer Mountains, 36
Kit Fox Warrior society, 83

L

Lakota people. *See also* Crazy Horse
    Black Hills and, 42
    Fort Laramie Treaty of 1851 and, 38
    Little Bighorn and, 24–26
    tribal groups and, 23
    warfare and, 14, 15–16
    Wounded Knee and, 123–124, 127–128
Lame Deer, 26, 106–107
Lame White Man, 26, 81, 88–89, 90
languages, 23, 64, 72, 122
Last Stand Hill, 8
Leigh, William Robinson, 138
Life with Custer (Whittaker), 131
Limber Bones, 89, 90
Lincoln, Abraham, 34
Little Big Man (Berger), 140
Little Bighorn National Battlefield Monument, 142–143
Little Bighorn village, description of, 22–27
Little Crow, 34, 35
Little Hawk, 45, 93
Little Muddy Creek, Battle of, 106
Little Rock, 99
Little Thunder, 31
Little Whirlwind, 89
Little Wolf, 44, 105
Long Knives, 45, 53
Longfellow, Henry Wadsworth, 133
Low Dog, 26, 59
Lower Brulé Reservation, 109

M

Mackenzie, Ranald S., 104–105
Makes Room, 86
Makhipiya-Luta. *See* Red Cloud
Makoce Sica, 114
Mankato, Minnesota, 34
map of Battle of the Little Bighorn,
　96
Marquis, Thomas B., 137–138, 139
Martin, John, 64–66, 72, 99
massacres, 10, 31, 36–38, 46, 100.
　See also Wounded Knee
McLaughlin, James, 110, 113–114
Medicine Lodge Coulee, 73
medicine men, 41, 109
Mendota, Treaty of, 33–34
metaphors, Custer as, 138–139
Michno, Gregory F., 142
Miles, Nelson A., 83, 104–107, 113,
　118, 126, 131
military posts, 28
Milk River, 39
Miller, David Humphreys, 139
Minneconjou band, 23, 26, 30–32,
　104, 121–122, 125
Minnesota Sioux Uprising, 34–35, 36
Mister Custer (Verne), 140–141
Monahsetah, 99
monuments, 142–143
Mormon Cow, War of, 31, 32
movies, 136–137, 138, 140
Moving Robe, 59, 70, 72
Mulligan, Richard, 140
music, 140–141
mutilation, 70, 72, 99

N

Nakota people, 23
Native Americans, 72
New Ulm, 34
Noisy Walking, 60, 89, 90
Nye-Cartwright Ridge, 75, 77,
　78–80

O

Office of Indian Affairs (OIA), 32,
　42, 108–109
Oglala Sioux, 23, 26, 29–30, 35–36.
　See also Crazy Horse

Ojibwa tribe, 22–23
Old Bear, 26
Old Black Moon, 68
One Bull, 62–63, 68, 74
One-Who-Walks-with-the-Stars,
　25
Oregon Trail, 28–29, 31–32, 36

P

Paha Sapa, 41–42, 103–104, 108
Paiute Indians, 43
Pawnee Indians, 105
Paxson, Edgar S., 134–135
Phil Kearny, Fort, 36
pictographs, 135, 136
Pine Ridge Reservation, 109, 113,
　116–118, 127
platoons, defined, 21
Platte River, 28, 35, 38
Porter, Henry R., 70
Porter, James, 84, 100
Powder River, 36, 44, 48, 105
Pretty White Buffalo, 59
Pte-San-Hunka. *See* White Bull

R

railroads, 38, 41
Rain in the Face, 26, 36, 89, 133,
　137–138
rations, 19, 109
Red Cloud, 35, 36, 116
Red Cloud Agency, 105–106, 107
Red Cloud's War, 35, 36–38
Red Feather, 74, 82
Red Horse, 26, 86, 135, 136
Red on Top, 26
Red Tomahawk, 114
Reed, Henry Armstrong, 52
religion, 15–16, 40–41, 109. *See also*
　Ghost Dance religion
Reno, Fort, 36
Reno, Marcus A., 49, 51–52, 56,
　58–61, 66–73, 131–133
Reno Hill, 70, 73, 75
repeating rifles, 53, 93
Roan Bear, 75
Roman Nose, 89
Rosebud, Battle of the, 43, 45, 49,
　54
Rosebud Creek, 45–46, 49, 106

Rosebud Reservation, 109, 112, 113
Runs the Enemy, 74, 82, 93, 97

S

Sans Arc band, 23–24, 26, 33, 104
Santee Sioux, 23, 26, 33–34
scalping, 16, 35
scapegoats, Marcus Reno as, 67
scouts
    Arapahos as, 28
    Arikara, 20–21, 58, 63, 68, 70
    Curley, 71
    Custer's strike force and, 50,
      53–55, 58
    death of, 72, 73
    Rosebud Creek and, 44–45
    war parties and, 19
2nd Cavalry regiment, 31–32
Second Seminole War, 30
Seven Council Fires, 23
7th Cavalry, 21–22, 48, 49, 52,
    125–126
Shave Head, 114
Sheridan, Philip, 42–44, 46, 48,
    103
Sherman, William Tecumseh,
    42–43, 48
Short Bull (Brulé), 112–114
Short Bull (Oglala), 66, 106
Sibley, Henry B., 34, 35–36
Sioux Nation, 12–16, 22, 28, 31, 32
Sioux wars, 34–38
Sitting Bull
    Big Foot and, 116
    Canada and, 40, 41, 104
    as celebrity, 109–110, 136–137,
      140
    Crazy Horse and, 46, 107–108
    death of, 114–115
    Ghost Dance and, 113–114
    life of, 24
    Little Bighorn village and, 26
    Reno's attack on, 58–60, 62–63
    Sioux wars and, 36
    Sun Dance vision of, 45
    surrender of, 35, 108

Slim Buttes, Battle of, 104
Smith, Algernon E., 75, 86, 89, 98
Smith, George M., 63
spiritual rituals, 16
Spotted Eagle, 26, 104
Springfield Carbines, 52–53, 93
Squaw Creek, 75, 81
Standing Bear, 59
Standing Rock Reservation, 109
Stony Lake, Battle of, 35–36
suicide, 90, 91
suicide boys, 60, 88–89, 90, 107
Sulley, Alfred, 35–36
Sumner, Edwin V., 116
Sun Dances, 26, 45, 109
Swift Bear, 63

T

Tashna Mani, 59, 70, 72
Tasunka Witko. *See* Crazy Horse
Tatanka Iyotanka. *See* Sitting Bull
tepees, description of, 24–26
Terry, Alfred H., 43–45, 48–49, 54,
    100–101
Teton Sioux. *See* Lakota people
They Died with Their Boots On, 98,
    138, 140
Thunder Hawk, 93
Treaty of Mendota, 33–34
Treaty of Traverse de Sioux, 33
Two Kettle band, 23, 26
Two Moon, 26, 44, 68, 83, 84,
    134

U

Upton, Emory, 21

V

Van de Water, Frederic, 137
Varnum, Charles A., 54–56,
    120–121, 127
Verne, Larry, 140–141

W

Wagon Box, 38
Wallace, George D., 125
war honors, 16, 24, 89
War of the Mormon Cow, 31, 32
warfare, Sioux Nation and,
    12–19

wascimum sapa, 69
Washita River, 10
wasichus, defined, 40, 41
Washita Massacre, 100
Water Carriers' Ravine, 100
wealth, buffalo and, 14
weapons, 13, 48–50, 52–53, 93, 120, 123
Weir, Thomas B., 82–83, 97, 100
Wells, Philip, 125
Western Sioux. *See* Lakota people
White Buffalo Calf Woman, 15–16
White Bull, 36, 59–60, 81–82, 86–90, 106–107
Whitestone Hill, 36
Whitside, Samuel M., 118–119
Whittaker, Frederick, 131
Wier Point, 64, 83
Wilson, Jack, 110–115

Wilson, Woodrow, 83
Windolph, Charles, 101
Wolf Mountain, 105
Wolf Tooth, 77–78
Wooden Leg, 69, 85–86, 90, 99, 137–138
Woodpecker Woman, 112
Woolaroc Museum, 138
Worm, 107
Wounded Knee, 115–128
Wovoka, 110–115

Y

Yanktonai Sioux, 23, 26
Yates, George W., 56, 75–78, 81, 95, 98
Yellow Bird, 121–122, 123
Yellow Nose, 76–77, 89
Young Black Moon, 63

About the Contributors

Author **MICHAEL L. LAWSON** is a historical consultant on Native American issues with Morgan, Angel & Associates, a public-policy consulting firm in Washington, D.C. He formerly was a historian with the Bureau of Indian Affairs and the Smithsonian Institution. He is the author of *Dammed Indians: The Pick-Sloan Plan and the Missouri River Sioux*. This book and additional research he conducted served as the factual basis for legislation awarding more than $380 million to five Sioux tribes in South Dakota and Nebraska. He holds a B.G.S. and an M.A. from the University of Nebraska at Omaha and a Ph.D. from the University of New Mexico. The Western History Association and the South Dakota State Historical Society have honored him for his writing on Sioux topics.

Series editor **PAUL C. ROSIER** received his Ph.D. in American history from the University of Rochester in 1998. Dr. Rosier currently serves as assistant professor of history at Villanova University, where he teaches Native American history, the environmental history of America, history of American Capitalism, and world history. He is the author of *Rebirth of the Blackfeet Nation, 1912–1954* (2001) and *Native American Issues* (2003). His next book, on post-World War II Native American politics, will be published by Harvard University Press in 2008. Dr. Rosier's work has also appeared in various journals, including the *Journal of American History*, the *American Indian Culture and Research Journal*, and the *Journal of American Ethnic History*.